Ultra-lite
Steelhead
Fishing

Ultra-lite
Steelhead Fishing

Ralph F. Quinn

ICS Books, Inc.
Merrillville, Indiana

Ultra-lite Steelhead Fishing

10 9 8 7 6 5 4 3 2 1

Printed in U.S.A.

Published By:

ICS Books, Inc.
1000 E. 80th Place
Merrillville, IN 46410

Library of Congress Cataloging-in-Publication Data

Quinn, Ralph F.
 Ultra-lite steelhead fishing.

 Includes index.
 1. Steelhead fishing. I. Title. II. Title:
Ultra-light steelhead fishing.
SH687.7Q56 1986   799.1'755   85-30586
ISBN 0-934802-26-2

DEDICATION

For the better part of a dozen years I've lived this book of UL Steelheading and now that it's complete I realize that without the help of my wife Joan much of it would not have been possible. Throughout she's been on the scene as fishing partner, photographer and when I was loaded with gear, a key grip. Many times in past seasons she has asked (jokingly of course) if she could . . . "just be my wife, not a fishing buddy." On more than one occasion she's pulled in the bacon when I failed, and I'm glad for that. More often than not she's a steadying influence, suggesting, questioning, and navigating when I lost the way. For her ready smile, dedicated ways and fishing skills I dedicate this work. Kudos to you JOAN!

Table of Contents

ACKNOWLEDGEMENTS

Like other books on the subject of angling much of the information contained therein has come through association with fishermen and so it is with Ultra-lite (UL) Steelheading. If it wouldn't have been for my early association with Lou Emelo I doubt if my trouting career would have ever seen the light of day. But it was my good fortune to be adopted by this dedicated hunter and fisherman.

From that first trip to central Pennsylvania's trout country in the late 50's, I've come to appreciate the skills needed to consistently fool all trout — browns, brooks and rainbows. Along the way I've been fortunate enough to come in contact with quality individuals who took the time to educate a quizative angler from northeastern Ohio.

In 1965 I moved to Michigan and shortly thereafter joined TROUT UNLIMITED. Through the Jackson Chapter of T.U. I met Howard Overmyer, an inventive and talented fly tier (of KEEL FLY and SWISHER/RICHARDS fly fame) from

Michigan Center. Howard influenced my fly tying immensely and with those skills I continued down the trouting path. Somewhere along the line (1968 or '69) steelheading caught my attention and I haven't been the same since.

For a time I bounced around the midwest chasing rainbows and finally I met pioneer light liner Dick Swan. Much of the information gained in those early days came from Dick, not so much by questioning, but by observation. Gary Marshall, formerly a Resource Specialist with the Michigan Travel Bureau, also helped expand my horizons. Matter of fact, Gary lent me his favorite "meat stick" (UL Steelheader) to land my first rainbow in the churning surf at Thompson Creek.

There were others who added significantly to the information pool, but one in particular, Mike VerBurkmoes, one of the fishing "Delinquents" mentioned in Chapter 1, offered more than his share. Thompson Creek, Rogue River, Tippy Dam, Elk River, Big and Little Manistee meetings kept the UL story flowing and for that I am grateful.

Recent associations with Dick Pobst of the Thornapple Orvis Shop Ada, Michigan and Dick Smith, a class act flyrodder from Lowell, Michigan, put the stonefly angle in perspective and the information contained in the "selective steelheading" section came from outings with both anglers.

Finally, I wish to thank my brother Lou Quinn for standing in when I needed an acting steelheader. The same goes for Brian Alber, a quality person from Grand Rapids, Michigan.

PREFACE

All of this began, I suspect, more than thirty years ago in the unlikely place of southwestern Florida, amid salt flats, breakers and seagulls — bonefish country if you will. I'd come from a fishing family, so I fell into the madness legitimately. In the early days (late 40's) my father, then a Civil Service employee, was stationed at Drew Field, Tampa, Florida, so my older brothers Pete and Roy and I were summarily baptized in the briny reaches of the Gulf of Mexico. By six, I was an old pro on common ocean species like flounder, sea trout and yellow jack, yet, the fresh water world was but a remote entity, a picture on the barbershop calendar.

I don't recall the exact circumstances surrounding my first foray inland (I think it probably involved three whining boys demanding to "fish somewhere else"), but somehow the bequest was granted and off we trudged. The locale my dad selected was a camp on a remote, back-country portion of the Hillsborough River, and appropriate enough it was called Trails End." It was here and later on the St. Johns River that my fishing career took a turn for the better. Bream and bass in the clear waters of these streams made a lasting impression on me, and it's continued into the present.

When we moved north (Ohio) in the 1950's, I thought my fishing days were over, but I was pleasantly wrong. Dad didn't show much interest in pursuing the lesser fresh water species, so it was left to brother Pete to show the way. By now he had his drivers license and with that "wonderful" instrument, plus a rickety, '48 Chevy coupe, we were able to ply the major rivers of northeastern Ohio. The target fish there was the smallmouth bass. Most of the rivers in this unglaciated section of the Buckeye Country ran clean and pure. Away from the ravages of strip mine operations, we found excellent populations of bass, and I guess it was these experiences that whet my appetite for the ultimate of fresh-water species — stream TROUT.

As a teenager, I developed an insatiable need to read about and purse these finny denizens, and at every opportunity, I cut, studied and filed articles devoted to the subject. When I look back on those early readings, It's easy to see why my quest took on grand proportions. Among the authors were the elite of the angling fraternity: A. J. McClane, Ray Bergman, Wynn Davis, Joe Brooks, Jason Lucas, Lee Wulff, etc. Even though I had never drifted a line for trout, I felt like a seasoned veteran. All I needed was a chance. Now enter one Lou Emelo, and the trouting saga of R. F. Quinn takes a positive turn — one that's brought me in contact with nearly every major species of Salmonid.

If there's a word to describe my mentors trouting philosophy, it's DEDICATION. Lou Emelo cut his teeth brookies in the tumbling mountain streams of central Pennsylvania, and even though he plugged an occasional bass lake in Ohio's Columbiana Country, Lou's first love was trout. A chance meeting on a local reservoir, and my brother Pete and I finally found a direction. "McConnell's Mills, Pennsylvania, has a good trout program each spring," Lou commented. "Why don't you work on your first trout there, then give me a call. If you are interested, I'll be headed for

Trout Creek, Salmon Creek, Slate Run in PA. next month. You might want to tag along."

With an invitation like that I graciously accepted, then began counting the days. To make a long story brief, brother Pete and I cleaned up along the gravel and boulder-strewn banks of the Mills. The ticket there was single salmon eggs, drifted on bottom, or in the white-water eddies, mid-stream. Of course those first fish were hatchery reared, but they were trout in all their glory. Their olive backs and crimson stripes were etched so strongly in my memory that thirty years later I can recall those creeled rainbows like it was only yesterday.

That same June, I tagged along with Emelo and per his plan we pursued rainbows and brown trout in central Pennsylvania. I continued to drift single eggs and garden hackle, but when we arrived at Slate Run, Lycoming Co., near Renovo, PA., it was flyfishing only. I was shocked to learn that I couldn't pursue trout with more simplistic methods, but it forced me to channel my efforts in another direction. Lou Emelo was an accomplished flytier and caster, so I became the student once again.

I watched and learned. Slowly at first, but by the end of the season I'd made up important ground. I purchased a flytying outfit from the now defunct Herter's Inc. Waseca, Minnesota, and went to work. The following spring I was an accomplished tier and flycaster, even though the formula for catching on wasn't very clear. I also assembled an 8 foot light action flyrod to round out the picture. If nothing more, I looked the part of the "trouter," rod to creel.

It was during my second season that I really learned the ropes of river trouting. The location was the upper stretches of the Kinzua Creek, near Kane, Pennsylvania. It was May and instead of gullible rainbows, I was after brown trout. Lou felt it was time I ate a little humble pie, so off we splashed. The gin clear-waters of the South Branch didn't help the cause. I caught a few browns on fly tackle, but I had to fall back on bottom-bouncing with single eggs and minnows to get big trout interested. I never did hook, let alone land one of these brutes, yet I was learning the lies and feeding lanes stream trout used.

On my third trip to Kane, I was toting a, then new, concept in trout taking tactics. It was a UL spinning rod and matching reel. I'd taken the hint from an article A. J. McClane published, entitled "Hair Lining Trout" and built a willowy rod from the upper two-thirds of a progressive, light action flyrod blank. Now, I'd have the edge on browns. Basically, that prediction was correct. I upped my percentages on trout hooked and landed, but the big ones evaded my best efforts.

Through my college years at Bowling Green State University, Bowling Green, Ohio, and into the mid 1960's, I continued treks to the Keystone State with Emelo and brother Pete. When the angling situation called for it, I used fly tackle. Otherwise, I drifted naturals. I wasn't a purist by any means. Ultimately each tactic complimented the other, and I was able to satisfy basic questions on stream trouting which, until then had gone unanswered, particularly on nymphing (both naturals and artificials). My pride and joy remained the UL concept, however, and when I moved to the Great Lakes State, Michigan, in 1965 to work on my Masters Degree in Biology, this technique ultimately payed off big with River Steelhead. But, I'm getting ahead of the story.

My first trouting seasons in Michigan were entirely directed toward flyfishing legendary rivers, such like the Au Sable, Pere Marquette, Big Two-Hearted, etc. I felt like a young lion crusading for truth in trouting. I did extremely well on these Classic Waters, basically because I'd specialized in Aquatic Zoology in my Master's program, plus I tied up with trouters who knew the rivers well, particularly the correct time to wade them. "Matching the Hatch" was more than simply identifying mayflies. Timing, I found, was everything in trouting — a valuable lesson for the last part of this tale.

I think it was 1967 or '68 that Michigan's steelhead program got on track in a big way. In the early years, nearly every major river draining the Great Lakes State, north, south, east, west, was full of mighty rainbows. The steelhead was back in force. I read a number of articles expounding the fishery as a "Boom" proposition, so 1968 was my baptism into the ranks of Rainbow pursuers, and I haven't stopped chasing them since, spring, summer or fall.

Initially, I worked spring-run, spawning fish with flyrods, and although I caught steelhead, the down time between specimens was longer than I wanted. Solving the problem of the "Mystery Fish," or "Silver Bullet" (as steelhead are affectionately called in the Midwest) came largely through studying the pioneering efforts of Stan Lievense, a Fisheries Biologist, specializing in trout lakes, formerly of Lansing, Michigan, now Traverse City.

Stan was a long time aficionado of the big anadromous rainbows and when he couldn't strike paydirt (even though fish were visible) he theorized that the water must be the culprit. "Forty-five degrees is the magic temperature at which steelhead become very active," said Stan during a steelheading seminar in Grand Rapids. "Below this temperature, the species are temperamental and difficult to catch." I remembered those words as I probed my favorite steelhead river (the Pere Marquette River) spring, 1968, yet I still experienced tough going.

In those "early poor" days, nearly all of my steelheading efforts were something less than spectacular. Occasionally, I'd land a pair of fish in a weekend of hard angling, but more often than not, I came home empty handed. Why? I attributed it to fisherman pressure. When I did take/hook into fish, they usually came in early morning, before the army of anglers hit the stream, so resting the quarry had a lot to do with success. Yet, there were times when conditions were ideal and no fish were landed. Why?

Carrying the pressure theme one step further, line pound-test seemed to make a difference. Light leaders certainly produced more fish per hour than heavy tippets, but keeping the fish on was another problem. Old style steelhead rods, stiff butts and active tips didn't handle rampaging rainbows very well. Old time pros realized this long ago and opted for lighter blanks for their steelheading efforts.

It's tough to pin the label on the first steelheaders employing long rods and light leaders for taking lake-run rainbows, but two names certainly come to mind, Dick Swan Clare, Michigan and his long-time fishing amigo, Ellis McColly, Midland. Dick and Ellis worked their magic in the late 60's at the old Homestead Dam site, Betsie River, and clearly showed that line-shy steelhead could be consistently hooked on light leaders, but keeping them on was another story.

Recalling, those early UL steelhead rods were simply flyrod blanks rigged with spinning guides, but within months after the long rod concept got going in the Great Lakes, several rod manufacturers began producing/building blanks exclusively for Light Lining. Lamiglas cooked up a batch of blanks in the 9 to 12 foot range. Loomis was quick to follow with Light Progressive actions. The rest is history. I acquired my first blank from Lamiglas in 1975, and I've been pointing the butt at steelhead ever since.

Those early trouting days in Pennsylvania served me well on my initial quest for Light Lining River Steelhead. I had the bottom bouncing technique down. Terminal setups came through association with anglers in the know. The tackle/gear was available for those willing to roll their own, so early on, the die was cast. Every season since, spring and fall, I've hooked more than my share of rainbows (averaging over 50 to 80 fish since 1971), but bringing them to hand is another story. Typically, I land 15 to 20 percent on 4 pound-test. Half that on 2 pound and with 6 pound, I might break the 40% mark. As one sage trouting expert put it, "It's better to have hooked and lost than not to have hooked at all." I agree.

Making the adjustment from standard steelhead tackle to Ultralight methods takes some finesse, but with patience and dedication, I feel the average angler can make the switch. If you're an old-time trouter, the route to successful light lining is just a short hop. For the beginner, a keen eye and observing nature will put you there quicker. There are no short cuts to successful steelheading, but from where I sit, Lightlining has to shorten the path. It did for me. It can for you.

Figure 1.   The steelhead embodies all that's wild and mystical in nature, making him one of the most sought after trophies in fresh water.

CHAPTER 1
EARLY EXPERIENCES —
PRE-ULTRALIGHT

Wild, mystical and a brawler in the finest sense of the word, the steelhead — *Salmo gairdneri* — is the acknowledged King of the trout family across the U.S. and Canada. Mention him to the easterner and he's synonymous with placid lakes and deep water trolling. To the midwesterner and Great Lakes fisherman, steelhead mean long rods, fine leaders and drifting baits. To the west coast angler, he brings forth remembrances of wobbling spoons, turbulent rivers, stiff rods and spectacular scenery.

To each angler, steelhead are many fish, not just a single species. He's adaptable and to catch him you must fit angling tactics and techniques to his habitat. Nowhere is this fact more evident than in the rivers and creeks draining both coasts of Michigan's lower peninsula. Here, with an ever growing army of fishermen each season, the steelheader has been forced to change strategies or go fishless. But, change didn't come easily.

In the early days, pre-1964, before the eradication of the sea lamprey from Great Lakes waters, the ritual of western steelheading — stiff rods, heavy leaders and golf-ball size baits, was dropped on the angling public. Accounts of giant sea-run rainbows were carried in the big 3 outdoor publications and they flatly stated . . . "to land one of these bruisers the trouter must use hefty equipment or forget it." The public took the copy as gospel, further entrenching the broom handle tackle philosophy.

Ask any old time steelheader (since 1965) to show a typical terminal rig and chances are good the setup will consist of a pencil lead assembly, with trailing Mustad hook, size 4 or 6. Of course these outfits take fish, yet for each one hooked many more spurn the offerings. Herein lies the question? Do you, as an angler, want to engage few fish and be 100% assured of landing them or hook many steelhead and by using skill and technique land more, perhaps a limit each time out? That's the dilemma I faced fourteen years ago, and I opted for the latter. But I was lucky.

Early Ultra Light Days

When I began serious pursuit of lake-run rainbows, back in 1968, technology was on my side. Rod manufacturers were just beginning to experiment with a vast array of space-age materials: i.e. Graphite, high modulus fiberglass, plus graphite and glass blends, etc. The problem with most of the "new" generation tackle centered on design. Without exception, rods were designated "medium" to "medium heavy" for strong-arm tactics — thus the enigma of days gone by continued to cloud and confuse the issue. Now, enter the custom rod builder.

As with all outdoor endeavors, there are few among the masses that seek to enhance and extend their favorite pursuits and steelheaders are no exception. The goal with these individualists is simple, catch more fish and do it with greater consistency than ever before!

Although it's debatable what year the revolution in midwestern steelhead tackle began, away from standard gear toward ultralight, but 1967 seems as likely as any. For shortly after that date Dick Swan and his angling associate from Midland, Michigan, Ellis McColly started working on a series of solid glass "bike" rod blanks (the same fiberglass stick used for bicycle flags) as the basis for creating the "ultimate" steelhead rod. After one year of prototype designs, the pair of experts were ready for the acid test.

The location chosen was the old Holmstead Dam site on the Betsie River, near Benzonia, Michigan. It was spring, mid-April and the annual push of spawning rainbows was well underway. The sky overhead was clouded, but by 10:30 a.m. the sun broke through, warming the tumbling currents.

Within moments after Swan began drifting his fragile leader he shouted, "Fish On," and the line of huddled fishermen made way. Minutes passed and Dick beached a sleek 6 pound female. Fifteen minutes later, Ellis followed suit, and so the morning went. By days end (5:30 p.m.) the duo had hooked 19 fish, landing 6. Nothing special about that you say. Perhaps? But when you consider they were the only ones hooking and landing fish all day, that says a great deal about the fishermen, and the tackle they were using.

From those austere, grass-root beginnings, a dedicated following took hold, and the "Michigan" technique of light leaders and long rods, for migrating steelhead became a part of angling history. Two or three seasons went by before commercial interests noticed the light line crowd, but notice they did. Realizing there was an ever growing market out there just waiting to be taped, several blank manufacturers jumped into the fray.

Lamiglas was the first of the majors to produce glass for both custom and commercial markets. Heddon saw the light at the end of the tunnel and introduced a quality ultralight glass rod for a relatively modest price. The heart of Heddon's effort was a light, progressive action flyrod blank and fishermen welcomed it with open arms. Fenwick came on board in 1975. More recently, 1981, Daiwa introduced a series of long rods into the growing commercial market. Cabela's, the mail order house based in Sidney, Nebraska, added a graphite noodle rod in 1983 and the design looks promising for the carbon fiber fan. Success breeds success

Figure 2. Pioneer light liner Dick Swan shows late season steelhead from Michigan's Elk River.

and with the recent introduction of World Class light monos by Stren and Berkley, it's predicted that by the late 1980's most established rod manufacturers will have a light, long entry for steelheaders, east, midwest and west.

Why? Because they work. It's that simple. To make the point stick, here's another tale of standard vs. ultralight tackle.

Again, the story involves pioneering light-liner, Dick Swan and his group of angling Delinquents. It was July 13th, 1978, and Washington's famous Toutle River (devastated by Mt. St. Helens in 1981) was flowing smooth, cold and wild. Summer steelhead were a new experience for most of the Michigan anglers, but after a spectacular morning of gyrating silver torpedos, they felt like natives. Five fishermen hooked 17 fish, 9 were beached.

Their success was dwarfed by the giant Douglas firs surrounding the Toutle and the clan simply walked away from the river "pleased." It wasn't until Washington steelheading expert Jack Ayearst revealed . . . "the average northwest steelheader lands but two steelhead per season," that their "success" took on added significance. During the three weeks of west coast angling that followed, Swan's gang tallied 158 hours of fishing and in that time hooked 144 rainbows, 38 were landed.

When you examine the west coast steelheaders tackle, it isn't tough to see why they hook so few sea-run rainbows. Again, stiff rods are the rule, rather than the exception. Rigging is typically heavy-duty, tube/pencil sinkers and trailing gobs of bait. Leader poundage is 8, 10 to 15 pounds, sometimes higher. The philosophy being, hook two fish a season, land two fish a season. And, they do. But for sport?

Regardless of steelheading geographics, I doubt if there's an experienced angler that will argue with the affect of heavy rods and leaders on angling success. Clear water, large baits and suspicious fish don't help hooking ratios one bit. Even wild fish shy away from such clothesline tactics. Yet, the standard steelheader argues their system works on both big and little rivers, and I suspect they are right, at least part of the time. But, over the entire season, spring, fall, winter, you can bet on the light liner.

With both limited time and season to pursue steelhead, it only makes sense to go the ultralight route. With the percentage of returning rainbows numbering in the 40 to 50% range (for both planted and spawned steelhead) plus an ever increasing army of pursuers, it's just good business to use tackle that will up your ratio of "fish on." The way I see it, I'm willing to give up a few fish from broken leaders and bend the rod more, than wait hours, days and sometimes weeks between strikes.

During a recent Steelheading gathering in southwestern Michigan, I had a well known Canadian fishing guide tell me . . . "when I go steelheading now, with UL tackle, I have much more confidence that I'll hook fish than ever before, particularly when using standard lures and gear. The Ultra Light thing is a whole new ball game and frankly I don't know why I didn't latch onto it sooner."

Over the last four years, the number of light liners on midwestern streams and west coast rivers has increased ten fold, and all I can say is "welcome." There's always room at the top for the enterprising "novice." The tackle is in place. The techniques proven. All that's needed is a redirection of "skills" and a whole new world of river steelheading awaits you. Hopefully, as you continue to read and experiment afield, the target will become clearer and clearer. It did for me.

Pre-Ultra Light — The Early Days

When the boom in Michigan's river steelheading took place in the late 60's, 1968 to be exact, I was a babe in the woods in terms of How To and Where To on anadromous rainbows. Not that I didn't have the interest. Far from it. But, I had become so immersed in flyrodding and Matching the Hatch aspect of trouting that I totally ignored the explosion in silver. That is until I received a phone call from an avid steelheader and flyrodder from Bellaire, Michigan, Tom Naumes.

"The Platte River is just about wall to wall fish right now, so if you want to try out that new rod, I suggest you get up here, pronto. I hooked seven fish yesterday and landed three. You'll be able to do as well." With such an invitation what fisherman could resist.

When Naumes and I waded upstream the morning of April 21st, 1969, a gray, cold mist hung above the river. Overnight the weather changed and an icy Canadian front pushed into upper Lake Michigan bringing rain and snow squalls. Tom's enthusiasm was at a high as we worked upstream. Ten minutes later, I was probing a stewn log known locally as the Doctor's Hole.

Steelheading, although not an entirely new experience, was strange with fly tackle. But, with Tom's sure guidance, I quickly adapted to the task. My rod was a medium-heavy progressive action Lamiglas blank designed to handle 10 weight lines. The reel was a single action Breaudux loaded with 150 yards of 15 pound-test back and a Wet Cel sinker. An 8 pound-test leader and No. 6 Skykomish pattern finished the rig.

Shortly after daybreak, Tom hooked and landed a four pound female. An hour later, a 3 pound male hit the bank and the action ended. "Too much light on the water," Tom observed. "You may as well hang it up for now, or until mid-day, when we can put the sneak on the jog jams. Here I was, rigged for bear and the fishing was over!

"You mean I drove five hours to fish two, then, "hopefully" we might hit something in the afternoon?" I quizzed. "There has to be a better way for the weekender to get some rod time!" As the story ended, I failed to connect. Matter of fact, it took two more springs on the Platte before I finally landed, not one but two steelhead! My victory, however, was a little overshadowed by the steady stream of bait fishermen who waddled the cedar-lined banks, loaded with silver fish. There had to be a better way!

The following spring I discovered *the* steelheading tactic or so I thought at the time. The locale was a gravel run below the Clay Banks section of the Pere Marquette River near Baldwin, Michigan. I'd been pounding the gin clear water since daylight. I had several fish in front of me, but no luck.

Dozens of casts and several fly changes and I backed off. That's when things got interesting. While resting the redd another steelheader waded downstream. Being a gentleman, I let the chap fish through.

I don't recall how many casts the guy made, but in minutes his long, amber rod began pulsating. The silver fish gyrated into the crisp April air and ploughed a path downstream. This angler followed. With net in hand, I brought up the rear. I wanted to be of service to the lucky stiff, plus see the "bait" being used on that spinning outfit. Spin tackle on fly only waters didn't seem right to me.

Ten minutes later, the steelhead careened into calmer waters below the run. The slender rod dictated the end, and I slid the wide-hooped net under the heavy fish and waded shoreward.

"What did that fish take," I questioned. There was a long pause as the angler dug into his vest. "A number 6 Spring Wiggler," he replied. "I've plenty, you're welcome to one."

Clutching the fly, I waved a fond farewell and headed for my camper. An hour session at the tying table and I'd mimicked the chartreuse bodied nymph perfectly. I was ready for action.

I rigged the setup identically. A three-way swivel, a dropper weight of 3, No. 4 split shot and a five foot leader terminating with the magic fly. I fished the same runs I'd hit earlier that morning, but came up empty. The flyrod was the problem.

Casting the rig was awkward. Accuracy, impossible and the sinking line didn't help. So, I retreated to higher ground.

That Wednesday, April 7th, I returned to the P.M. and the story changed. Armed with an open-face spinning reel and an 8 foot medium-light action spinning rod, I was able to probe the river, systematically and with little effort. By 11:00, I'd lost most of the nymphs, but I'd hooked five fish, landing one. Things were beginning to look up.

Figure 3. Author shows early fly-caught steelhead from Mich's Pere Marquette River. Rig was awkward to cast.

With angling/steelheading tactics in place, I made rapid progress in hooking lake-run rainbows. From a low of two fish in the spring of 1969, I landed 25 fish the following spring from rivers draining the west coast of Michigan's lower peninsula. Why the dramatic rise in success?

Part of the success can be directly attributed to the easy access to steelhead lies. With monofilament, I was able to accurately probe the river's bottom. For consistent hooking of steelhead, this is extremely important. Put your offering in the target zone and you at least stand a chance.

Another factor was the drag free drift. With flyline there wasn't a direct link between fish and strike, so I'm sure more steelhead were missed simply because the "take" wasn't noticed. When a steelhead mouths a bait there's usually a momentary hesitation in the drift, little more. Recognition of this often means the different between bending rods and slack lines. With monofilament line drag is minimal. When a fish takes, you know it.

No, I didn't suffer flyrod withdrawal symptoms. Long ago, I recognized the value of each tactic, and when one strategy didn't work, I'd opt for the other. On midwestern rivers many flyrodders increase their knowledge of a streams' currents by loading a spare spool with monofilament only. Purists swoon at the very thought of such an act, but again, if it gets the offering in the target zone efficiently and consistently — great. Fish will follow. Guaranteed.

It wasn't until the fall of 1975 that I really got into the flow of the light lining story. At the time, I was bumping around the Upper Peninsula trying to waylay an early run of Alaskan Coho that had been planted in the diminutive waters of Thompson Creek, near the village of Thompson Schoolcraft County.

After a long summer, most steelheaders view the pilgrimage as the beginning of the season on rainbows in the Great Lake State. Old home week had brought the long rod crowd out in force and when I began probing the charging waves at the top of Lake Michigan, I was determined to make the trip count. By 9:00 a.m. the action had ended and I

Figure 4. Expert steelheader Gary Marshall and "football" rainbow taken from Thompson Creek surf.

waded ashore. There, I struck up a conversation with a tall, weathered chap and it happened to be the grand dad of the Lite Liners, Dick Swan. He'd taken a stocky female from the grey waters that morning, and I wanted to know about his long rod and surfing setup.

"Your rod's too short, your leaders stout and you're rigged all wrong," Swan commented. "That can be fixed," he chuckled, "but we'll have to wait for the morning."

At daybreak, I launched a skein of steelhead spawn into the reflective waters of the rivermouth and waited. The rod Dick put in my hands was a 9 1/2 foot light action model, he called a "meatstick." Compared to my equipment it was a willow in the wind.

The lineup of anglers gradually expanded until it reached a submerged sand spit, some 100 yards to my left. Occasionally someone in the crowd shouted "fish on," and the lines gave way. I was totally immersed in the ritual when my line drew taunt. Wham! Twenty yards out a silver bullet boiled the surface, then raced right. "Fish On," I shouted. The strike was sudden and sure. Now, the only thing that remained was landing the prize. With a open arena and no snags, what could go wrong?

The steelhead ploughed lakeward. I brought it back. The slender glass bucked, but the 4 pound-test leader held. By the time I got a good look at the rainbow, 10 minutes had lapsed. This was a new experience for me. A prolonged battle simply gave the fish an advantage. With need-sharp teeth broad body and tail, any angler is lucky to win such a contest.

With some coaching, I slid the football-proportioned rainbow into Dick's waiting net. Swan just grinned and continued his vigil. When the action ended at 10:30 a.m., I'd gone three for three. The trio of steelhead pulled the scale down an even 25 pounds. Not bad for an amateur. I tried to relieve the rod from Swan's inventory, but had to settle for a second days use. When I returned home two days later I found a rod tube at my door. Inside, the short note read . . . "Here's a blank to work on. When you're finished, show up

at Tippy Dam. Action starts around November 15th. You'll
need real finesse there. 2 pound-test only! Ha! Good Luck."
Signed — D.S.

Since my initial plunge into the ranks of the light liner,
I've spent hour after enjoyable hour drifting, plying and
probing our river systems and charging waves for the *Salmo
gairdneri* — the mighty steelhead. At times the UL tactic is
nothing short of magic. When all else fails, fine leaders and a
well executed drift will take fish. But, alas, there are times
when even the best of the clan is left empty. The best thing
now is to pack your rod and take a break, but don't throw in
the towel. Steelheading is a challenging sport, and to
succeed you have to rise to the occasion in both patience
and strategy. Anything less (traditional or UL) is short-
changing the sport.

Figure 5. Savage nature of steelhead shows in swollen kype of male.
When hooked his rush for freedom is both powerful and calculated.

CHAPTER 2
THE TARGET FISH —
STEELHEAD AN OVERVIEW

Taxonomically, the giant, native race of salmonid known as steelhead is actually a rainbow trout, one step away from its home, the vast Pacific, or in the Midwests' Great Lakes — Michigan, Huron, Superior, Ontario. A steelie remains a steelhead only in the rivers of his hatching. When the species is transplanted to other waters it quickly reverts to rainbow ancestry. This is clearly delineated when *gairdneri* proceeds up rivers in spring, spawning time. Now, many black spots show on his sides and a red lateral band appears. Even though the trout resembles the nonmigratory form, that's where the similarity ends.

Steelhead have a hungry look. Big waters give *gairdneri* a savage nature. In males the jaw curves and its eye takes on the glint of a foraging predator, ready to take on the vast supplies of baitfish known as greenling or alewife in fresh water. Within three years of entering the salt or fresh water lakes, steelhead return to their imprinted river and it's here the angler feels his fierce character. When hooked, the steelie rushes pell-mell downstream and if this initial surge doesn't free the hook, his catapulting, tumbling, rolling and twisting leap for freedom just may do the job.

It's been more than 15 years since I first encountered this somewhat frightening phenomenon, but I can remember it like yesterday. A drawn out battle on light leaders is at once memorable and soul-filling. No previous freshwater encounter could have prepared me for my first steelhead, because he is indeed the King of the trout family. Long may he thrive.

A thumbnail sketch of the steelies life cycle in western and midwest streams shows distinctly different behavior patterns. To catch on, an angler should know when and what species are available, otherwise, the task of landing that first wild rainbow may be formidable.

On western, Pacific waters, for instance, steelhead can be found returning from the ocean in any month in the year. Those entering freshwater six months to a year later are known as spring or summer fish. Those entering spawning waters in the fall or winter (from December to May) are called winter fish. Winter fish are the most widely distributed — summer strains are relatively few in number. Steelhead entering the Columbia River passing above the Bonneville Dam are spring or summer fish. Oregon, Washington, and California have summer run fish, yet the fall species dominate.

Typically, the big rainbows enter northwestern rivers during late autumn, full of spawn or milt ready to renew the species. A heavy surge of water initiates the run and the steelhead moves constantly, until spawning redds are reached in headwater streams. These "winter" fish are highly sought, simply because they are feeding fish, for unlike the fasting salmon entering fresh water to spawn, the steelhead strike with a vengeance. Summer fish aren't much different. These trout are at the peak of life and their spawn is just developing. They feed ravenously and rise to both fly and bait regularly. Summer run fish enter rivers starting in

May, and at the time are a full year away from breeding. While it is true that winter fish are much larger, summer fish fight like possessed demons, with soaring leaps of 5 to 6 feet common.

Great Lakes steelhead/rainbows are a different story. Nationwide, anglers think of steelies as fall spawners, yet those in the midwest are strictly spring spawners (the exception is the *Skamania* strain of rainbow currently planted by Indiana in Lake Michigan which enters streams in June but do not spawn, Michigan introduced the same strain in limited numbers in 1984, returns are not in). Although initial brood stocks came from western sources, successive generations have lost the fall migration instinct.

After a long, hot summer, most of the streams and rivers draining into the Great Lakes system are far too warm to attract steelhead. In mid to late fall, however, cool nights drop river temperatures into the 50's, and rainbows begin congregating at rivermouths. By late October/November, river waters are once again comfortable and with an additional influx of early winter rains, the rainbows push upriver. This advance run is termed a "false spawn" by fisheries biologists. Why this phenomenon occurs is open to speculation. Some observers insist the movement is triggered by salmon migrations and the steelhead is doing what comes naturally. Others point to innate genetic traits inherited from past generations. Whatever the case, this fall migration provides excellent steelheading in many Great Lakes Rivers, with the additional bonus of rampaging salmon (kings, silvers), the run is much anticipated.

By December, early January, most of these fall fish are still in the rivers, particularly those large streams with deep holding water. Midwest rivers like Michigan's Big Manistee, St. Joe and Au Sable, plus New York's famous Salmon River are productive throughout January and February. As long as the rivers remain open, steelhead can be taken.

Once spring rains warm river waters, steelhead are on the move again. Occasionally, a mild winter hits and for the steelheader willing to brave cold waters, excellent angling

Figure 6. Trio of rainbows taken from Michigan's St. Joe River in February. If rivers are open steelhead can be taken.

can be had with few or no competing rods.

It's during this October run the biggest males enter river waters. The heaviest migrations, however, come in late winter and early spring, beginning in February over much of the Great Lakes. The initial push enters rivers in late February and March. By month end (March) a second run is underway and by mid April a third ascent has begun. This isn't a hard and fast rule, but three migrations are standard for big rivers draining, both upper and lower Great Lakes. Matter of fact, there are a number of streams in Michigan's northeast (lower peninsula), and Upper Peninsula, which produce excellent steelheading right up to and beyond Labor Day. Knowing this, the rainbow pursuer can have the best of two worlds — steelhead and warm weather!

As steelhead move up river, they continually use the same migratory routes, holding waters (runs, glides and holes) and spawning redds, season after season. Unless floods or ice jams change the river bed, these paths remain the same — old timers realize this and work hard to locate these productive lies. How? By constant fishing and observation. Informed experts, plus knowledgeable beginners (by trial and error) can usually look a strange river over and pick out the best riffles, runs and pools to ply their offerings.

Submerged structure (ledges, rocks and logs) is revealed by surface disturbances, flow rate, etc. Correct interpretation (reading currents) is a key factor in avoiding unproductive waters and concentrating on points where steelhead are found. For example, some stretches of water are too fast for trout to maintain themselves, so they move on. Dead water is usually a poor producer, but below Hydro Dams these regions can be very productive. If fished properly. We'll cover this aspect/angle in a later chapter. Same with water types and how to read them. For now, suffice to say that steelies prefer slicks above rapids and long uniform flows of moderate speed to tumbling currents, but again, there are exceptions.

After the advance groups of rainbow arrive in headwater regions, feeding instincts, although dulled, are put on the back burner. Spawning activities dominate now. Since most steelhead rivers contain limited spawning habitat, there's keen competition for these areas. The ideal redd area consists of gravel, fist to pea size, with a moderate flow of .25 to 3.1 fps. Quite often both steelhead and salmon select the same spawning gravel, so it's possible to observe one, and by accurately noting these locations, an angler can accurately probe a stream or river, even during high water.

Initially, females select the nesting site (the continuation of several nests constitute a redd). Usually, redds are placed at the head of a swift riffle, the lower end of a pool or in mid-stream, between or behind obstructions, submerged rocks or logs. Rapidly moving her tail and body against the stream bed, the female digs a shallow depression. Eggs are deposited in the nest, and in concert with an addressing male, they're fertilized. If water quality and stream velocity are suitable for incubation, the eggs hatch in 90 to 120 days, depending on water temperature.

The newly hatched sac fry spend one year in the stream then head for open water. During this "imprinting" period the diminutive rainbows acquire feeding habits which ultimately help the light liner take fish. I'll discuss these tactics in Chapter 4—Bottom Drifting and Chapter 5 —Mayfly Nymphs.

Once in Pacific salt or the Great Lakes, steelhead go on a feeding rampage. The major forage is a small baitfish similar to an anchovy or smelt. In 18 to 24 months the rainbow puts on a phenomenal number of pounds, averaging 8 to 10, with an occasional specimen weighing 15, sometimes more. Rapid growth on a high protein diet shows in the rainbows physiognomy, characterized by a small head and deep body. Steelheaders call these fish "slabies" or "footballs" and rightfully so.

After these overweight bullets hit parent waters they slim down. Fisheries biologists tell us migration and spawning stresses reduce body weight of both male and female by one-third. If you net an 8 pounder in upstream waters, at the lake/ocean the rainbow weighed 12. If you're

Figure 7.   Ideal redd area is smooth gravel with moderate flow. Females select site, males fertilize eggs.

determined to set a steelhead record, hit the rivermouth regions. That way, you'll stand a chance.

With survival rates of wild, stream-bred steelhead dropping or in some cases nonexistent (both coasts) Fisheries Divisions (midwest & west) have opted the hatchery route to replenish steelhead stocks. In Michigan, for instance, the DNR strips eggs from wild steelies, fertilizes in vetro, then hatches them in battery jars. Once the fry reach smolt stage (3 inches), they are planted in major rivers statewide.

This artifical breeding from one site (the Little Manistee Weir near Stronach, Michigan) has prompted true believers to condemn such hatchery practices, stating flatly . . . "steelhead have lost their zip, and the gene pool is inferior." I don't agree. If it's a choice between having good to excellent steelhead runs through artificial propagation or having poor to mediocre returns by natural reproduction, I'll choose the former. With the possible exception of watersheds in British Columbia and Alaska, the Great Lakes has, by far the greatest concentration of catchable steelhead on Earth. What more could the dedicated follower want?

With literally thousands of adult steelhead in front of anglers, why then doesn't success ratios soar? There are a number of reasons, but perhaps the biggest culprit is water temperature. As mentioned earlier, when steelhead enter parent waters, their focus is spawning, little else. Instinctively, however, they'll take up stream lies which direct drifting morsels their way. When water temperatures are in the mid to high 30's, a rainbows' physiology is at a low ebb. Movement from a stable lie to mouth a drifting bait now is unlikely, so the steelie sulks.

Every spring I keep a steelheading log, and if one factor stands between success and failure, water temperature is it. Here's a brief example. Spring '84, April 2nd to be exact, I was on the Muskegon River below Croton Dam near Newaygo, Michigan. When I began probing the gray currents at 5:30 a.m., water temperatures registered a chilly 38 degrees F. After an hour and nearly a hundred drifts, I

Figure 8. Check water tempertures constantly. One or two degree
change can bring steelhead to life.

hadn't turned a fish. Shortly, I waded ashore to warm my weary bones and await the sunrise.

At 8:30 the gates at Croton opened and with the influx of "warmer" lake waters, stream temperatures rose into the low 40's. Another hour and brilliant sunlight nudged the thermometer three more degrees. Whala! The steelhead began moving. At 10 o'clock, the mercury read a comfortable 46 degrees. From past experience, I knew something would break loose soon. All around my position the big rainbows porpoised freely. Most were competing males, so I knotted a Black Bear, Green Butt pattern, No. 8 to the 4 pound-test tippet and went to work.

Seven drifts and I was into my first steelhead of 1984, a crimson-sided male fresh from Lake Michigan. By 11:30, I'd hooked eight fish, landing three. All were bright as newly minted dimes and full of fight. Water temperature, plus the phase of spawning activity, put me in the success column. Since I began logging fish and water temperatures back in 1972, I've repeatedly run into similar circumstances, so the next time the action is slack on your favorite river don't blame the fish entirely.

Each spring I come across steelheaders who wale the water for a period of time, and finding no action leave. Yet within a couple of hours, the stream comes thumping to life. Steelhead in redd areas can be taken consistently, if the angler is in the target zone (bottom), and running the correct offering.

Behaviorally, the female is the focus of all reproductive activity. Spook or remove her from the redd, and spawning will ebb or quit all together. Take the male, however, and the ritual continues. Although, no angler is capable of choosing which sex he'll hook, he can be very selective as to whether or not the fish is released.

You and I have both run into this situation. Early morning and you're probing a gravel area. The bait, a mini-spawn sac the size of a garden pea. A dozen drifts or less and you're into a silver fish. Minutes pass and you slide a sleek female into the waiting net.

String the fish or release her? I've done both, but the

latter will prolong the angling period. Shortly after releasing the female, she'll head for the redd and continue pounding gravel. I've observed this phenomenon many times. You have too. Reorganization may take a few minutes, but during the wait, you may hook a male that's dropped into a deep run, pool or other downstream cover.

If pressure in the redd area is intense and light levels up, most self-respecting steelhead take refuge from the disturbances. That's why it's important to hit the stream early — shortly after daybreak, if possible. Of the consistently successful light liners I know, most are early risers. Sometimes you'll hurry, then have to wait for water temperatures to rise, but with increased competition, it just makes good sense to give it your best shot.

Shortly after migrating steelhead enter spawning water their coloration changes drastically. Once silver, the back takes on a dark olive hue, speckled with dark spots. The sides, plus operculum are flushed with a crimson iridescence of grand proportions. The gaudy coloration is part of courtship coloration, but the neutral tones serve as camouflage, protecting the species, particularly the female, from predators. Every spring I'm surprised by a female who, after being disturbed, has moved to the dark, unpolished section of the redd, upstream. It's natural for the female to move here, rather than leave the spawning area. Even the most observant, polarized eye finds it tough if not impossible to spot the target, but chances are good she'll be there. I've taken many of these sulking fish in the middle of the day, with a brilliant sun pounding the rivers surface. You can do the same.

Not long ago, a well meaning, but angle-minded scribe wrote a piece on the art of stone tossing to reveal a steelhead's (or salmon) presence. Shortly after that copy hit the newstands, I observed "fishermen" tossing rocks at redd areas, hoping to spot the female as she darted for cover. I'm sure the tactic works; but why do it? When a redd area is empty, probe the area immediately in front of the polished gravel. You may be pleasantly surprised.

Figure 9. Bright fish indicate migration has begun. This male took fly below Croton Dam, Muskegon River.

On many midwestern and western steelhead rivers, (particularly shallow, headwater spawning waters) rainbows are pressured so much during daylight hours, they've resorted to pounding gravel after dark. On the Pere Marquette River, near Baldwin, Michigan, for instance, this phenomenon has taken hold, and from what I can tell, it's here to stay. The only consistently productive tactic on the P.M. is to probe lies/redds well before daybreak and after sunset or hang it up. Pressure on this gin-clear stream is intense through the day, and the fish sense their vulnerability. In the headwater, Flys Only Section (M 37 Bridge to Gleason's Landing) steelhead disperse shortly after daybreak and don't reorganize until darkness settles over the river.

This behavioral change has brought about a new breed of steelheader on the P.M. Night-time angling is common practice here, but it's a weird brand of flyfishing. There's something strange about drifting flies or spawn (downstream waters only) in the dark. Everything is done by feel and repetition. Usually the angler takes up a position adjacent to a redd area or holding water and awaits darkness. When a fish is hooked it's contained in a given stretch of river or it's broken off. Wading after a rampaging rainbow in the dark and over strange bottoms isn't exactly my cup of tea, but the method works.

Spawning complete most river steelhead drop into the downstream holes to rest. This is where a carefully drifted spawn bag, fly or wiggler will take a specimen or two, but you have to be on target. These fish, although feeding, only mouth the offering. If they don't fancy the offering, it's rejected and fast. It takes expert technique and quick reflexes to nail these finicky feeders, so close attention to both drift and line tension is essential.

Before ending this segment, I'd like to comment on two controversial steelheading philosophies — Catch and Release angling and Fishing the Redds. For a number of years now, the light liner (midwest and west) has been maligned by a small, but vocal segment of the angling

Figure 10.   Proper release of played out fish insures survival. Hold steelhead by tall, gently support fish underneath, allowing water to flow through gills.

community for releasing fish that are "totally" played out. They contend light lining techniques force an angler to completely exhaust a rainbow before landing, and it's this very tactic that causes the premature demise of many steelhead, spring and fall. Conversely, they argue that using traditional tactics and tackle, a steelhead is landed quickly and surely, thus preserving vital energy needed to maintain the fish in cold waters. Result: the species has a greater chance at survival.

From personal observation of literally hundreds of steelhead taken by light line tactics, I have never seen a single mortality due to "overplaying." Steelhead are tough, resilient trout. If landed, handled and released properly, there's little likelihood of death through exhaustion.

The second question is a matter of tradition. Among west coast anglers the fishing of steelhead redds is considered taboo and a person doing so is guilty of committing murder in the fish degree — in effect killing the goose that lays the golden egg. I would agree to such a restrictive philosophy, *if* the practice would assure the restoration of wild fish stocks to the catchable numbers. Yet, alas, it can not. Even in steelheading strongholds such as Washington State and Oregon, rivers that once supported wild fisheries have, in recent years, declined in quality to a point where "hatchery fish" or put and take steelheading is a way of life. By fishing redds will midwestern steelheaders eventually eliminate a true American — the wild steelhead? I think not. In the Great Lakes State, for instance, we have quality rivers that continue to pump out hundreds if not thousands of wild steelhead annually (up to 50% of returning fish in the Pere Marquette are river spawned) yet many of these streams are open to year-round fishing, plus anglers here work the redds exclusively. Think about it.

If anything, the steelhead's worst enemy is mother nature. According to Neg Fogle, Anadromous Fish Specialist with Michigan's Department of Natural Resources, the mortality rate among first year returnees (3 to 5 yr. old fish) is between 40 to 60%. If the species survive, male or female to

return the second year, death rates can be as high as 80 to
90%. Aging, fungus, man-made hazards such as gill nets,
pesticides, chemicals, etc. deplete steelhead stocks at a rate
greater than all angling pressure put together. Whether or
not an angler/trouter decides to fish redds or try light lining
should be based solely on the merits of the program/tactic,
rather than a time-worn philosophy/statistic voiced by a few
anglers. To Catch and Release or To Fish Redds are personal
judgments that should be approached with both knowledge
and sensitivity, then decided upon. To do less is slighting
both the quarry and the Sport of Steelheading.

CHAPTER 3
BOTTOM BOUNCING BAITS

Every season (spring and fall) hundreds of thousands of the big, brawny fish known as steelhead orient to coastal rivers across North America like invisible guide-posts, and unerringly navigate to parental headwaters. Thus, renewing an event as old as the ages. Although fisheries experts are not in total agreement as to the exact mechanism triggering a steelies' migration into spawning waters, it's pretty safe to assume the phenomenon is innate, and a river's physical nature: i.e. odor, water-pressure, taste and perhaps temperature was imprinted on the sac fry as it developed in protective bottom covers. In the weeks following hatching, those immatures who survived the ravages of mother nature sought out these sheltered niches, further imprinting the bottom strata as home.

Here the developing rainbows found food. Micro-organisms for sac fry; nymphs, insects and late hatched fry for fingerlings. As these "parr" (named for the vertical marks

31

on their sides) reach estuarial waters, they take on the silvery color characteristic of the species. In this form, the brightly colored fish is called a "smolt," and he's nearly ready for the vast Pacific Ocean or the fresh water of the Great Lakes. Now, the steelhead ventures briefly into open water to feed and rest, yet he still maintains a strong affinity to bottom structure, i.e. bars, troughs, sand spits in river mouths, etc. Finally, after a year or two (depending on developmental stage) the rainbow moves lakeward or seaward to feast on its bounty, mature and grow into the migratory form we call *steelhead.*

When an adult steelie returns to the region of its hatching or planting three years later, and as it travels coastal waters attempting to identify a river as its own, *gairdneri* continues to navigate or orient to bottom strata. Reverting to earlier "imprinted" days, the steelhead moves upstream to renew the species.

For trouters after these migratory rainbows the tactic is simple. Ply the offering "on bottom" or "near bottom," that's where the action is. Season after season specific pools, riffles and runs consistenty yield steelhead to anglers who learn productive lies and put their baits/lures in the target zone. On the west coast, for instance, "strawberries" (egg clusters) worms, crabs, nymphs or spoons and spinners are drifted just off-bottom, using a three-way swivel, short leader and length of "pencil lead" for weight. In the Midwest, the rig is similar, yet the leader is lengthened, the three-way refined, and the lead is replaced with split shot on a dropper. The target zone is the same however, bottom or near there.

Actually, the term bottom bouncing is a little misleading, so some clarification is needed. When probing a suspected lie the goal is to "tick" bottom throughout the drift. By adjusting dropper weight and casting angle you can not only put the offering on bottom, but gain a drag-free drift — both important to success. Remember, the leader, hook and bait are simply along for the ride.

If your leader is short, the area covered is small, and more drifts are needed to probe an area. On the other hand,

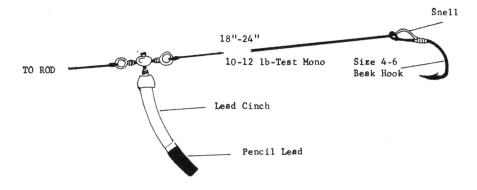

Snell

18"-24"

10-12 lb-Test Mono

Size 4-6
Beak Hook

TO ROD

Lead Cinch

Pencil Lead

Figure 11.   Typical west cost terminal rig is short and heavy, dictating strong arm tactics.

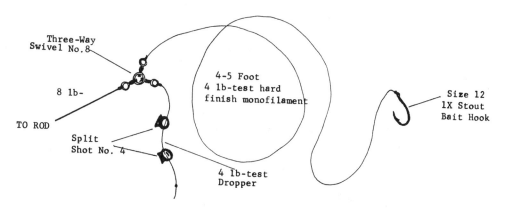

Three-Way
Swivel No. 8

4-5 Foot
4 lb-test hard
finish monofilament

8 lb-

Size 12
1X Stout
Bait Hook

TO ROD

Split
Shot No. 4

4 lb-test
Dropper

Figure 12.   Light line setup is refined with long, fragile leader, dropper weight and requires finesse fishing.

if the leader is long, a larger target zone can be covered. It's these long, "searching" leaders which make the "lite-liners" technique so effective. Handling such rigs requires the steelheader to use a long rod, thus the outsized sticks/rods in the 10 to 14 foot range. There are other reasons for using such tackle, but we'll cover those in Chapter 4 — Methods and Tackle. For now we'll restrict our conversation to the Why's and How To's of Bottom Bouncing Baits.

To approach this topic logically, it might be wise for the steelheader to first consider the phase or stage of spawning/breeding the rainbows are in — that way he'll be able to: 1. match his bottom bouncing tactic and bait to the season. 2. rig according to both water type and season. Otherwise, the wait between strikes could be long and frustrating.

Essentially, we can separate the steelheading season into three distinct periods: a. Pre-season b. Spawning and c. Post-season. Behaviorally, migrating rainbows have distinct preferences as to bait, lures during each period, and if the steelheader follows the migration closely, his chances for success are increased measurably.

As mentioned in Chapter 1 — Target Fish-The Steelhead, initial migratory urges hit Great Lakes rainbows sometime in late February (fall-October, November for west coast steelhead) and shortly thereafter, the giant trout begin gathering off river mouths, anticipating the push into headwater regions. Now, the steelie is fit, silver and full of fight. Warm estuarial waters attract the species in sizeable numbers and with an influx of spring/fall rains the run begins.

These steelhead are essentially feeding fish, so the wise bait choice now is fresh skeins of salmon eggs or raw spawn (Great Lakes parlence) drifted in river mouths or the deep holding waters further upstream. Instinctively the species recognize such fare, and a carefully executed drift will produce fish. When I say carefully executed, I mean on bottom and on target. In cold water, steelhead will not move to mouth a drifting bait. You must hit him right on the nose.

Keeping your offering on bottom requires a short leader compared to mid-season/spawning rigs. Typically, the nylon is 3 feet and since early season fish are unsophisticated — that is, they're not line/leader-shy and are feeding, an angler can use sufficient poundage to get the job done. For "lite-liners," this means 6 pound-test in limp varieties of monofilament. Four pound-test in hard finish, tough brands. Since most holding waters — runs, glides and deep holes — have snag-covered bottoms, it makes good sense to use a leader that's capable of stopping a rampaging steelhead.

Another top bait for pre-season fish is a spawn mimic made of soft plastic similar to that used in bass worms. They come in a variety of hues and sizes, anywhere from clusters, mini clusters to single eggs. The biggest advantage of phoney spawn is its durability, outlasting the traditional hand-tied sacs 100 to 1. Its drawback is the buoyancy encountered. When your weight is operating on bottom, the bait is well above the target zone. In mid-season this "handicap" is very desirable, but early, it could mean the difference between a big zero and "fish on."

Pre-season fish are also suckers for a well presented mayfly nymph like *Hexagenia limbata* or similar large burrowing *Ephemerid nymphs.* Through their "imprinting" days, young steelhead make a good living feeding on aquatic insects and nymphs, so the mix with adults makes sense.

While pre-season rainbows typically grab a drifting spawn sac, the take with nymphs is little more than a hesitation. Recognizing these "strikes" will be easier, if the angler runs a short leader, and mainline slack is kept to a minimum. That way, there's a direct route to the feeding fish. If an opportunity is missed, continue drifting, paying particular attention to the point where line and water meets.

After water temperatures rise into the 38-42 degree range, steelhead occupy headwater/spawning gravel, and it's here that light lining techniques shine. Typically, steelhead select redd areas 1 to 4 foot deep — ideal for spotting targets, but poison for anglers using traditional tactics.

Figure 13.   Top bait for spring steelhead is plastic spawn, both clusters and single eggs. Have a variety of colors on hand.

Heavy, leaders and thin water pose a threat to all steelhead. A few passes with strong-arm setups, and the rainbows will vacate the area, returning only after the threat has ended.

If you're a long-time steelheader, I'm sure you've encountered a situation similar to the one below. It's daybreak and you're rigged with 6 or 8 pound-test. A dozen drifts through the redd and you hook a female. Ten minutes later the steelhead is landed, and you go back to work. Drift after drift, is rejected. It's 9:30 now. Light levels are up, and you can't buy a steelhead. Through your polaroids you occasionally spot a steelhead, yet all action has seemingly ended.

Under such demanding conditions, the smart angler refines his rig, dropping to 4 pound-test and lengthening the leader to 5 feet, or more. For instance, if I'm using a 10 1/2 foot rod designed to handle 2-6 pound-test, I adjust the length to 5 1/2 foot, and continue drifting. The three-way swivel, although operating some distance from the fish, is also refined. Why? Using the "threat" theory as basis, small is less noticeable, thus less threatening. Hook size would also be changed. If you're running a No. 8 or 10 drop to a 12 or 14 wide bend hook, like Eagle Claw's No. 42 or similar. That way, you'll achieve your goal (refinement) and still have sufficient hooking/holding power.

Even though spawning steelhead are essentially non-feeding fish, they do strike/mouth lures, baits, flies and do it consistently, if the offering is presented in the least threatening manner. Translated, this means long, light, clear leaders in the 2 to 4 pound-test range. These so-called "searching" leaders are effective, because they probe several zones through a single drift. At any point through its path, the bait can be taken. Keep a close eye on the mono, and you'll be ready to set the hook. There are times when an addressing, secondary male hooks itself, and in doing so, "catches" the fisherman, but don't count on it.

Bait/lure selection in mid-season is entirely personal. I doubt a steelhead will reject your offering, if it's drifted at the right level and time of day. In my experience steelies are most receptive just after daybreak or during mid-day periods, after water temperatures rise and disturbances die down. Angling pressure has an adverse affect on rainbows, so an early start should help put you in the success column.

As the second and third wave of migrating steelhead hit redd areas (late March to mid April) spawning activity intensifies. During this period several males may attempt to mate with a single female and it's these secondary, addressing males we're interested in. Again, these fish are non-feeding, but will strike a well delivered, lure or fly on light leaders. My favorite is a dun-gray stonefly pattern, Size 8, 2x long.

Steelhead, particularly those in redd areas, often encounter nymphs of the large, black stonefly, *Pteronarcys*. Most are dislodged as the female digs its shallow gravel nest. Below the redd area competing males pick up these drifting nymphs, not because they are feeding, but out of instinct, and I suspect to terminate the threat posed. I'll cover the art of "selective steelheading" in detail during Chapter 6 — Trouting with Flies. Sufficient to say now that in the right hands, Flies are deadly.

As the season moves into the post spawning period, most steelhead have completed reproductive tasks and begin drifting slowly toward open water. With energy levels low, the fish occupy river lies which permit both feeding and resting. Holes, deep runs and glides are ideal points for the lite-liner to explore using exciter tactics (plugs and lures). Done properly, the tactic is truly spectacular, if not awesome.

This style of steelheading was pioneered on west coast rivers by the crew and staff at Luhr Jensen, headed by Buzz Ramzey. Matter of fact, Jensen named the technique after one of the lures they market under the trade name "Hotshot." Essentially it's a deep lipped diver which probes a stream's bottom in an enticing, darting motion. If the plug nudges a rainbow in mid-current, the results are both immediate and explosive. Smashing strikes are common using Exciter methods, and by using long-shock absorbing rods and light leaders the fish can be landed. Other exciter

Figure 14.   Diving lures Excite steelhead into striking and are popular choices during Fall & Winter season in Midwest.

lures used by steelheaders include flatfish, tadpollies, and the larger versions of Spin-n-Glos (winged bobbers), Wobble Glos, etc.

It's been more than fifteen years since the Exciter brand of steelheading hit the midwest. At that time Emel Dean, a guide from Bear Lake, Michigan, began pulling plugs in the swift currents of the Big Manistee River below Tippy Dam, near Brethern. His tactic became known as the "Drop Back" method of steelheading. Actually, the technique is bottom bouncing using lures and in Dean's case, the plug is either a U-20 Flatfish, silver or a magnum Tadpolly. Depending on current speed and time of year, the boat is anchored above a steelhead hole and the lines (usually 4) are played out. Fifteen yards to start, then extended five foot at a time, until the entire run or hole is covered. If a steelhead is resting nearby, he doesn't stay idle long, smashing the lure in one savage blow. If the line holds the battle ensues somewhere downriver. I'll cover variations of this tactic in Chapter 9 — Boating River Steelhead.

As with other forms of freshwater angling, exceptions to established rules are common, and so it is with steelheading. There are periods throughout the season pre, mid and post, when the angler can do no wrong. Seemingly every drift yields a writhing steelhead, and limit catches are the rule rather than exception. However, with the high rod pressures encountered today, such phenomena show less and less. I can recall the last "hot" steelheading session I participated in and to date, it hasn't been equalled.

The location was the Rogue River, near the town of Rockford, Michigan (a suburb of Grand Rapids, S.W. lower peninsula). It was April 17th, 1977, and per usual water conditions below the Childsdale Dam were high and turbulent. Heavy rains and sleet had pelted the tributary a full week and the color of the stream resembled coffee with double cream. When I began probing the tailrace section below the dam, it was 6:30 a.m. Already the line of anglers numbered a dozen or more, with more coming.

I quickly knotted a No. 12 wide bend bait hook to the 6 pound-test leader, hung a hot pink plastic nugget and went to work. Three or four drifts and my slender glass rod pulsated to the beat of a silvery steelhead. Within minutes the fish turned downstream. There, the fish slid into a side current and the long rod dictated the end. I strung the fish and headed into the fray once again. By 7:30 I had my limit of gleaming beauties, but so did everyone else. The real eye opener was the variety of baits the steelhead jumped on.

The guy next to me was using, of all things, night crawlers. I remember him saying . . . "if they'll eat plastic, they'll eat anything." Others floated phoney spawn similar to mine. While others drifted fluffy balls of yarn snelled to short shank bait hooks, Size 4! Another chap ran a popular walleye bait known locally as a walleye womper, but in this instance, it became a steelie bopper! I couldn't have been more pleased for all the steelheaders that day. Everyone took fish — long rods, short rods and in-between rods. But, alas, the action only lasted two days. The hord of steelhead remained in the stream, but with clearing conditions tough fishing returned. From there on out, the "lite liners" showed the way.

Since that spring day eight years ago, I've run into success ratios on other rivers similar to those encountered on the Rogue, yet only those trouters sporting long rods and light leaders have stood out. The heavy line, leader and rod steelheader takes fish, now and again, but consistency is the "lite-liners" forte. Bottom bouncing the UL way is finesse fishing — steelheading. Catch it, and you too will join the ranks of successful rainbow chasers, now and in the future.

Figure 15. Top steelheader Lou Quinn took this prime fish during high water on Michigan's Rogue River.

CHAPTER 4
BOTTOM DRIFTING —
TACKLE AND TACTICS

"Show me a trouter who can read a river, put his bait on bottom and I'll show you a successful steelheader." Even though the above statement isn't attributed to an Angling Guru or Rainbow Potentate, it does embody the essence of the steelheading experience. Back in the early 60's, veteran west coast flyrodder Ken McLeod made a comment that dovetails with this basic concept, so I think it's worth repeating. "The truth is," Ken wrote, "some steelhead will hit a fly at any time under reasonable water conditions in any month that steelhead are in the rivers . . . if the feathered counterfeits are fished properly." Of course these words are open to interpretation, but the observations "any month and fished properly" are the keys to the steelheaders enigma — fly, bait, light line or otherwise.

Steelheading in the midwest and west coast is typically a high water proposition, accompanied by turbid conditions. Spring melt and rains raise rivers to abnormal

43

levels, thus, the fisherman's/angler's problem is two-fold. First, he must find steelhead (knowing the fish is "on bottom" is just part of the problem) and second, he must use a bait or lure that will get the trouts' attention.

Finding steelhead. For the average rainbow chaser the answer is simple — follow the crowd. If the migration is in full swing and the angler plies his wares in known steelhead haunts, he catches on. Admittedly, the tactic puts ordinary fisherman into trout, but what about those pre and post season cases when steelhead utilize different stream lies? For trouters capable of reading a rivers' path, these periods still produce outstanding catches, regardless of river conditions. Five seasons ago, I had this point pushed home and I haven't forgotten the episode.

The story begins in early April, 1977, on Michigan's Rogue River, north of Grand Rapids (southwestern lower peninsula). Three years earlier, the Department of Natural Resources, as part of their urban steelhead program, planted nearly 3/4 million fall fingerlings in the Grand River System, including Prairie, Fish, Buck, Crockery, Sand Creeks plus the Rogue River. Surprisingly, these marginal plants took, and a hord of silver fish forced their way into the Rogue's headwaters near Rockford.

From late March to mid April untold numbers of steelhead were wrenched from the river's amber currents, then the rains came. Five days of monsoon-like conditions pelleted the watershed, and river rose to near flood levels... yet the fish continued to show. So did the fishermen, yet few caught fish. Occasionally the "crowd" rose to the occasion, not often, however. Why? Most were drifting their offerings in the wrong place!

With the influx of heavy rains, the steelhead abandoned traditional lies for calm waters shoreward. I didn't realize it until a "local" hooked a fish right off my boot tips. The real kicker was the fact he was fishing Behind a line of anglers who'd waded mid-river to "reach" the fish on the far bank. Under normal water levels the tactic would have worked, but not now. After the front line realized what was happening, they simply reversed their drifts 180 degrees. Shortly, they too began hooking fish.

On another occasion, I had a similar situation develop, but it was below the Grand River's 6th Street Dam, downtown Grand Rapids. Water levels, Spring 1979, were at an all time high, three to four feet above normal. At first glance it was tough to tell there was a retainer dam at the site, yet I knew better. In the pell-mell currents, steelhead had abandoned mid-river locations for the cushioned waters near the rocky shore. Taking a silver bullet here was easy. No drifting at all. Just "jig" an attractor, hot yarn fly behind a rock and wham? Fish On! Occasionally a bait chugger would hook a fish off-shore, but it required an ounce of lead to get down.

Unlike fishing visible targets, bottom bouncing baits for the most part, requires an angler probe areas where he only suspects steelhead. Some anglers call this tactic "blind" drifting, but it's far from that. Plunking down a bait or fly in the right location is 50% of hooking a steelhead. The remaining 50% (landing) is a combination of tackle, technique and skill. You'll experience more than your share of errors in the quest, yet I feel these trials are needed to develop a workable "Lite-Line" strategy. One can certainly learn a great deal by watching "resident" experts do their thing, but keep in mind, there are few shortcuts to consistent steelheading success, UL or otherwise.

As mentioned in Chapter 2 — Target Fish, steelhead select the same river lies season to season, and only by radical shifts in bottom topography will they adopt new positions. Recognizing these areas requires the steelheader read a stream's surface, then project this image to underlying strata.

There's no magic in reading water, just logic, based on experience. We know for instance, that water flowing through a channel having a smooth bottom, the surface will also be smooth. The speed on top is essentially the same as on bottom. Put a large stone in the channel and water deflects around it, forming a pocket of quiet holding/feeding water, above and below. If the stone is submerged, its presence can be detected since the object displaces a similar amount of water, creating a surface disturbance on the downstream side. Put a series of large stones in the channel and bottom currents are slowed, causing the surface to appear choppy or riffled.

If we visualize how an obstruction affects the bottom flow, we can also read how it slows, deflects or increases the rivers' current. These physical features help fish hide, feed, rest and they also serve as signposts to the angler — fish here.

Steelhead in pre-season are easy to find if you remember most prefer to lie in currents requiring minimal effort to maintain position. Deep pools and glides are prime examples. With sufficient water overhead, such points afford fish both food and protection and should be considered prime targets in early season.

As the migration continues and spawning gets underway, steelhead select gravel areas of uniform dimension (pea to fist size) flowing .08 to 3.18 fps, one to four feet deep. Again, these locales are easily recognized by their smooth surface waters. An even bottom translates into "potential" spawning habitat and should be systematically probed. Since females continually pound gravel, such areas appear lighter in color than the surrounding stream bed. A pair of polaroids help locate any fish redds, so keep them handy. Otherwise, you'll pass by a lot of steelhead and you will, indeed, be fishing blindly.

Water level, as mentioned earlier, is another important factor in selecting pre-season lies. During years of high, spring runoff, rivers become discolored. Under these conditions rainbows feel a greater sense of safety and often occupy stream positions that may be completely exposed during late May or early June — fine for the rainbows' survival, but a real headache for fishermen.

One of my favorite spots for spring steelheading is the Muskegon River near Newaygo, Michigan, but the river here is a tough nut to crack. The major problem is fluctuating water levels. Since the Muskegon's flow is controlled by

Croton Dam, there are times when it's almost impossible to get a bait on bottom, yet an hour later, the stream flows slowly, lower than low, similar to conditions in late summer.

While turbines are generating power at mid-day, steelhead actively spawn and feed in the current edges and it's a simple matter to hook fish right off your rod tip. But after five o'clock, the wheels grind to a halt. Water levels drop, and those same waters are literally empty. To catch on now, long casts and light leaders are a must. Like all trout, steelhead are concerned with safety first, and low water provides little protection.

When fishing rivers controlled by hydro dams, use low water periods to explore the area, making note of spawning gravel, obstructions and pockets which may attract migrating rainbows. Once water levels stabilize, I'm able to probe the lies accurately, thus avoiding unproductive bottoms. If your favorite river doesn't have a dam, investigate the area by boat or wait until low water periods of late summer. Believe me, the effort will be handsomely rewarded.

Big water steelheading is intimidating simply because these rivers are difficult to read. Remember, large streams are just blown up versions of smaller ones and follow a similar pattern of pools, riffles, glides and more pools. The shallow gravel stretches are its food factories. With a suitable velocity, they also become spawning regions for both steelhead and salmon. The heads of nearby rapids and tails of pools are also good bets for steelies, particularly during mid and late season. Since there are many examples of what constitutes good steelhead water — points and lies — I'll cover a number of these in later chapters, that way, you'll have some concrete examples to compare notes with and hopefully grow on. For now, lets get on with drifting our offering in the target zone — bottom.

Of the problems confronting steelheaders, proper terminal rigging is primary to catching fish. If done in a precise manner steelhead are not threatened. The "strike" or "take" follows and from there on, if we play our cards right, we'll land our prize.

The typical "lite-liner" setup is a simplistic affair consisting of a three-way swivel, dropper line, leader and hook (bait or fly). That's it. One eye of the swivel is knotted to the main line monofilament (usually 8 pound-test). The second gets a five inch dropper of four pound mono (for splitshot). The leader is attached to the third eyelet and we're ready for action.

How long should the leader be? And how much weight? This is determined by river level, clarity and velocity. The goal is to "sweep" the rig through suspected hangouts with the weight periodically ticking bottom. If not, pinch additional shot to the dropper. I use removable lead, that way the shot can be reused later.

When the rig hangs up, lift the rod tip slightly. The current smoothly "walks" the setup downstream, completing the drift. If the rig snags, a pull on the main line mono frees the outfit, with only the split shot lost. Each season I run into yards of stray monofilament left in my favorite runs by steelheaders using one poundage for leader, dropper and main line. By using dropper and leader pound-tests, one-half that of main line monos, this can be avoided. We have enough problems hooking and landing steelhead; why add another?

Basically, "lite-lining" is a more refined version of traditional steelheading methods, so terminal rigging should reflect this theme — swivel, shot, leader and hook. Use a No. 8 three-way, but if No. 10's can be located run them. Shot sizes, No. 4's first, then No. 7's. At times 0's are needed to get on bottom, yet these weights are tough to handle on UL tackle (1-4 lb-test). When mid-river lies require 3/4 oz. of lead, select a heavier stick (2-8 lb-test) or wait for lower water. That way, less gear is lost and when a fish is hooked, you stand a chance of bringing it back.

Since the hook is the important link between you and that prized steelhead, select it wisely. First, choose one that's classed 1x stout and needle-sharp. Actually, "striking" with

UL tackle amounts to lifting the rod, little more. This action alone should be sufficient to bury the barb. If not, consider another design. The ones preferred by 90% of Great Lakes "lite-liners" are the wide-bend hooks by Eagle Claw and Mustad, No.'s 42 and 37140. Both designs permit "hanging" the bait, with sufficient gap remaining to nail a feeding fish. Sizes 12 and 14 cover most situations, but there are times (high water) when Size 10 is better.

Leader length is adjusted to water levels, clarity and existing light factors. In early morning, when steelhead are most active, (due to reduced angling pressures) the standard is 3½ to 4 foot, 4 pound-test. From this point, the angler can go up or down depending on water and light levels. If waters are clear and normal, leader lengths should be increased to 5 or 6 feet. I generally don't go much beyond 7 feet, but reduce pound-test. Again, the idea is to lessen the threat to resting or spawning steelhead. By getting the lead, swivel away from the fish you stand a chance. Three, two and one pound leaders are "normal" under critical low-water conditions. If the fish are going to strike, this setup should be the ticket.

There is an ongoing debate among lite-liners concerning leader visibility and "Fish On." One faction contends clear monofilament is better than high visibility brands. While others say brown or camo green is the only way to go. At times, I suspect both groups are right. With so many variables affecting whether or not a fish is hooked, it's tough to tell what triggered the "take." I suggest using a leader (length and brand) that's produced in the past, and keep an open mind. Personally, I use opaque, clear monos throughout, and have excellent luck. Fish as though you mean it (concentrate on every drift) and you'll take steelhead.

Leader finish, i.e. hard vs. soft, limp vs. stiff, is another subject that gets considerable debate. I know ULers who use the hard, tough varieties and are very successful. Others tell me hard finishes, although abrasion resistant, don't have the knot strength, particularly in cold weather. In the other debate, limp vs. stiff leaders, arguments center on reduced drag factors, because "it (limp leaders) tends to flow with varying currents." It no doubt snakes through bottom currents better, but is it more effective in fooling steelhead?

All options considered, I prefer hard finish, low visibility lines. The tough surface is extremely durable, even in the 1 and 2 pound-test categories, IGFA Rated. During prolonged battles a steelhead's teeth come in contact with the leader many times, and over the long haul, hard finishes have landed more fish for me. They could for you.

Before leaving this topic, I'd like to consider one more aspect — searching leaders. Earlier, I mentioned the subject and stated that long, fine leaders are used by lite-liners to locate fish, when drifting "blind." I think this needs clarification.

If we start with a 3 to 4 foot leader, 4 pound-test and fail to hit fish, the logical course is to lengthen the mono and continue probing. By extending the leader, the angler can cover the water at varied depths. Steelhead, even in river currents, tend to stratify. That is, they hold at different levels, depending on temperature and clarity. For instance, in high, turbid waters, fish have their noses tucked right on bottom. Later, as river levels drop, these same fish suspend inches to feet off bottom. A long, searching leader moves our bait through current levels and "finds" resting fish, particularly in early and late season, but when fish are on the redds, a short leader is easier to present and control.

Handling these outsized, light leaders requires the steelheader to use a long rod. (Remembering, however, length alone is not the sole determinant on whether a rod is suited to handle light leaders). When I say long, obviously I'm referring to glass blanks in the 9½ to 11½ foot range, up to 14 foot. The action of these sticks varies with manufacturer, but most are classified slow (uniform flex tip to butt) to progressive, ultra-light (light butt, UL tip). The latter is essentially the design used in flyrod blanks, with less layering of glass. For instance, if a traditional 10 foot blank has 8 wraps on the mandrel, an UL blank of equal length has half that number.

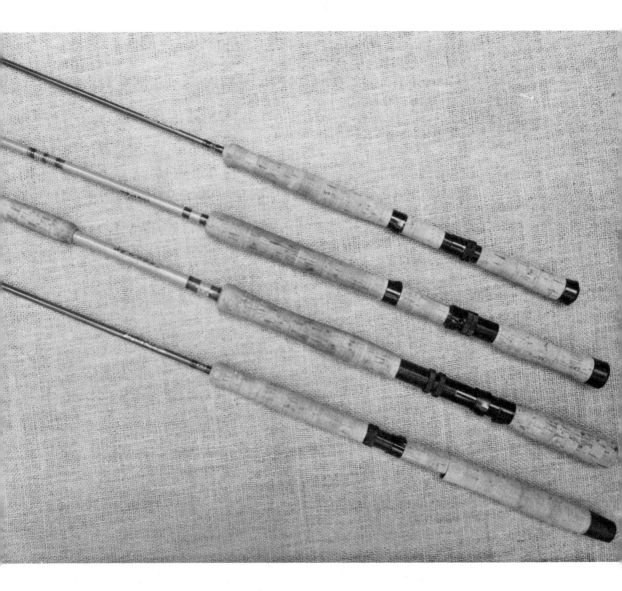

Figure 16. Tools of the trade — a lineup of UL rods. (L to R) Steel-header, 10 Ft; Light Surf'n Steelheader, 9½ Ft; Noodle Rod, 10 Ft; UL Flyrod, 9½ Ft. 4/5 line. (Note handles).

Wall thicknesses of commercial blanks vary so much today, it's difficult to tell whether or not the glass is capable of handling light leaders. If you're wondering whether that long rod you purchased is capable of handling light leaders, rig your outfit as outlined earlier, tie a 4 pound-test leader to a solid object and have at it. Pull the rod into a deep "C" bend, point the butt at the target (hook). If the leader holds, chances are good you'll be able to handle a moving fish/steelhead.

Most factory rods being produced today are classed UL. This means they'll handle a variety of line tests, 2# through 8#, 10#. The specs are written on the blank (above the foregrip). Watch for them.

The Custom rod is another story. The blanks used in these sticks are "cooked up" versions of factory glass, with the recipe supplied by the maker. There are "semi-custom" builders also. These guys use commercial glass and allow the customer to select guides, grips, reel seats, etc. In either case, the rods are expensive, often costing two to three times that of commercial makers. If you have the money and time, a custom rod may be in your future.

For aficionados, there's a specialized version of the Ultralight rod termed "noodle" or "bike." These blanks are designed strictly for 2# leaders and under. Most will double up under such frail monos and still hold together.

If you're fishing low water in late season or winter steelhead these rods are excellent, but during early and mid-season outings, when water levels are up, they just can't stop a rampaging rainbow. Like other forms of fresh water angling, suit the UL rod to the fish and water conditions, that way, you're in control.

The long rod, in addition to giving the steelheader an efficient fishing tool, allows the average angler to maintain a drag-free drift. Translated, this simply means more fish per hour. Years ago, flyrodders recognized the value of a long rod in pursuing trout with nymphs. All factors considered, nymphing with flies is very similar to bait fishing, in that you read the water (find the fish), then present the fly in such a manner that the feeding trout takes.

By using a long rod, the angler present his bait/offering with reduced drag or ideally, no drag at all. The major culprit in all drifting (bait or fly) is line drag. The extended glass keeps a large percentage of monofilament off the river surface — the result is a fish fooling drift.

Another long rod advantage is the small amount of mono needed to reach resting steelhead. With an 11 foot rod, for instance, an angler only needs to extend his cast 15 to 20 feet and he's able to probe lies within a 30 foot radius. On a short line the strike is relayed sooner, so theoretically, the fisherman can set the hook quicker. Remember, a steelhead inhales a drifting bait, and if it's phoney, rejection follows and FAST. This brief hesitation is our only clue to the "strike." A long rod gives us the time edge that translates into more "Fish On."

Additionally, long rods act as shock absorbers, thus the steelheader avoids loosing the fish in the opening minutes. Think about it. After hook-up, the rainbow typically goes through a series of rapid head shakes, terminating in a violent surface boil. If this maneuver doesn't lose the hook, the fish rushes up river, catapulting its silver body skyward. On traditional, stiff rods, such antics put extreme pressures on the leader and the hook usually pops free.

Of course, even the lite-liner should drop the rod tip when the steelhead surfaces. Once the fish's head is beneath the churning currents, however, the rod butt should be pointed at the target. By keeping constant pressure, the angler fights the fish every second. As long as the glass is in the Classic "Big C" bend, the steelhead must give way. Basically, it's a Law of Physics. The longer the lever, the greater the pressure/work that can be applied/completed. Translated into simplistic terms, a lot of heavy weight steelhead hit the shorelines every spring (and fall) and the tool responsible is the Ultralight rod.

When I began serious UL steelheading back in 1970, the standard reel for long rods was the closed-faced 1810 by Shakespeare (discontinued in 1980 and reissued as Spincast II, 86). Since then, a number of manufacturers have intro-

Figure 17. During battle UL anglers use Classic "Big C" bend to tire fish. Point butt toward target at all times.

duced similar models aimed at the UL market. Zebco has the Model 144 and 154. Daiwa recently introduced two lever operated reels, Model US 80 125M, which look promising. Garcia has the Fast Cast #1 and #2 and the list goes on. The closed-face spinning reel gets the most play, because it offers a number of advantages that open-face reels can't match. Yes, there is a movement away from the traditional, but I feel its origins are based on factors other than performance.

First, the closed-face reel is rear mounted, so the angler doesn't have his casting hand in contact with a metal reel seat. Since most steelheading is conducted in what can be termed "miserable" circumstances, this plus is worth it's weight in BTU's. A simple release of the internal bail and the angler is ready to cast. No fussing with external bails or wet monofilament. Anglers use open-face spin reels on rear mounted systems, yet the bail must still be triggered and proper line tension maintained. It can be done, but there's a lot of wasted motion. If you're accustomed to an open face, it just may be the one for you.

The biggest advantage of a closed-face is the ease in which extra mono can be "spilled" from the reel. Release the line pickup and lift the rod tip, that's it. As the mono slips through your fingers, length is easily controlled. Why spill line? While fishing a lie in mid-stream, it often becomes necessary to extend your drift to cover, for instance, the tail of a run or redd area. Steelhead hang in these spots resting, and extended drift puts your offering in front of these fish.

As the main line monofilament drags, spill line until the area is covered. If this means two rod lifts, fine. With the line under your control, any hesitation in the downstream drift is easily detected. An open-face reel can accomplish the same thing, but with more effort. Open or closed-face, select a reel with a butter-smooth drag that's easily adjusted — then you'll be able to handle heavyweight steelhead in close quarters.

Since both midwest and west coast steelhead waters are intensively fished, it's the angler's responsibility to spool his reels with monofilament that's 2 times heavier than

Figure 18. Open or closed-face, reels should have smooth drag and capable of spooling 150 yds., 8 lb-test. Author perfers enclosed spool for better line control.

leader pound-test. In other words, with 4 pound leaders, use 8 on the main line. Six pound leaders require 12 pound, and so on. Why double the pound-test?

If you're fishing properly, on bottom, hangups are inevitable. By running lighter weight leaders and dropper lines, only split shot and hooks are lost, not long streamers of heavy monofilament. Steelheaders have enough problems to worry about, without adding stray line to the drift lanes. Proper rigging can eliminate this "hangup" now and in the future . . . if everyone does their part.

At this point we've read the water, assembled the best outfit-rod, reel and terminal setup, now it's time to drift our offering and hook that silvery prize called STEELHEAD. By doing our homework and working methodically, the goal will be reached.

The key to successful drifting is repeated systematic casts, drifts and follow throughs. Accuracy is important, both distance and depth. Haphazard methods and random casting take steelhead now and then, yet over the long haul, attention to detail nets fish after fish.

Earlier I told a tale of wading steelheaders who misread a river's currents and until they reversed their drifts, nobody hooked fish. Season after season I watch fishermen lob and drift offerings in waters that are empty or continually probe an area where rainbows are present, yet never touch one. In the early days I was guilty of the same offense, but quickly learned my lesson.

The teacher was a rag-tag steelheader, who arrived late that April morning and since I was only going through the motions, I offered my spot in the procession. "No thanks," he replied, taking his place at the end of the lineup. "Such folly," I mused. "The fish are mid-current, half way up the run, 15 to 20 yards out. Where he's operating, he'll only get snags." A dozen drifts or so, and the weathered anglers' rod tip arched deeply. Snag, I thought. That's when a silver torpedo nearly hit my outstretched rod. "Fish," the steel-leader cried and after a brief battle upstream, the rain-bow careened into the main current. Following the fish down, our newcomer beached a sleek female in the 7 pound class. "Luck," I groaned. An hour later and three more fish, I took the hint and moved downstream. Drifting close, in the tag-end of the run, I quickly hooked and landed an 8 pound male. After that, the action ended. Light levels and pressure caused the fish to move, yet I'd learned a valuable lesson.

When pressured by drifting lines, steelhead occupy waters which afford both protection and calm. In the above case, this happened to be the end of the run, 10 yards out. Here, the rainbows found no leaders and a cushion of edge water to maintain their position.

Since the anglers first task is to find fish, every cast should be directed at methodically covering the area, top to bottom. Essentially, you want to broadcast a series of drifts across the target zone, then move. Or if your position is fixed, the cast can be adjusted, up or downstream.

If we've determined fish may be holding at position A (10 o'clock) three feet down, the cast should be directed upstream to point B (11 o'clock). Consider current speed, then adjust the dropper weight to allow your offering to "drift" through the suspected lie (Point A). You'll feel the shot "tick" bottom. If not, pinch additional lead to the dropper and direct your cast further upstream, to the 12 o'clock position. Some trial and error will be needed to find the correct drift combination.

As the main line swings through an arc, follow the drift with the rod tip. By pointing the tip at the bait, drag is reduced. Less drag gives your bait a natural, unattached look, plus, the strike, when and if it comes, is telegraphed much quicker. Every spring and fall I watch steelheaders direct casts across currents, only to hold their rods stationary. When the bait reaches a point downstream, they let it dangle in the tumbling currents. Admittedly, such tactics take fish, but for every steelhead hooked many reject the offering before the angler is aware.

Periodically, a hang-up occurs and after freeing, the angler cranks in his line. I used to do the same, but have since learned to complete every cast. On more than one occasion

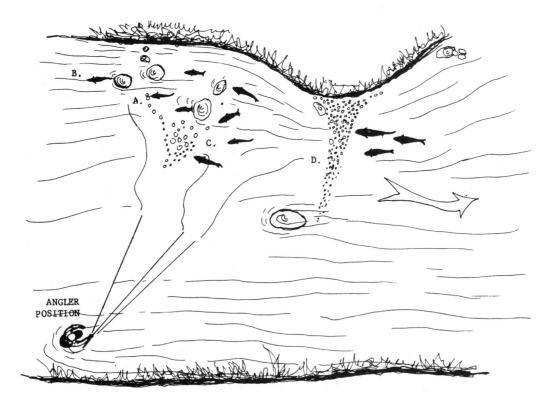

Figure 19. Cover suspected lies by overlapping drifts. Follow mono's progress with rod tip and keep bait on bottom.

I've pulled a bait free and had a resting steelhead pick it up, particularly after water temperatures reach the mid to high 40's.

The mechanics down, let's go through a drift sequence. Start with a series of casts directly in front of your position, progressing outward, to 20 or 30 feet. Lobing to Point A, follow the drift downstream, then swing the dropper further upstream. This way, you not only tick bottom quicker, but extend the target area.

After 10 to 15 casts, length the main-line mono to Point B and repeat the procedure. Then go to Point C, continuing until the area is blanketed. If a steelhead takes during the drift, determine where the "strike" came and continue drifting.

The ground covered, take a step downstream and continue the process. Occasionally, however, fishermen numbers restrict movement, then you'll have to rely on casting, plus line spilling to extend the drift area.

When the "strike" comes, it's little more than a hesitation, so watch the line carefully. Keep the rod tip at a 20 degree + angle, so there is a pronounced down slope to the line. Using a long rod, excess line is held from the rivers surface and drag is reduced. The result is a more direct hooking route.

From time to time the leader runs into spawning or resting steelhead, the fisherman reacts, foul hooking the trout. "Lined" fish typically launch into an immediate series of catapulting leaps and race downstream. If this happens, point the rod at the target and with an in-line pull, break the leader. There are times, however, when a fish hooks itself, rockets skyward, and somehow becomes entangled in the leader. The steelhead looks fouled, but isn't. Suspecting this, drop the rod tip and kick out additional monofilament. Hydraulic drag is quickly brought into play. The resistance appears to be coming from downstream, the rainbow heads upstream, hopefully freeing the leader. Regain the lost line and with a little finesse you should be able to determine the course of the battle.

Throughout the protracted contest point the butt cap directly at the fish. That way, the steelhead is under constant, unrelenting pressure. Using the "shock absorbing" quality of an UL rod, it's tough to break 4 pound-test monofilament. Most steelhead are lost at the rod tip, simply because "stretch" in both main line monofilament and leader is gone. When stress comes, the fragile leader takes the entire load.

There's another reason why steelhead are lost in the closing seconds and it centers on the 3 way-swivel rig. As fish tire, the tendency is to lift the rod tip and direct the quarry into the waiting net. With heavy leaders and stiff rods this tactic works, but on UL tackle it's poison. Once the dropper line, shot and swivel leave the river, a pendulum action is set up, swinging the leader back and forth. When the fish rolls, this side to side movement becomes more violent, and the hook is literally "tossed" from the steelheads' mouth.

In the early days I lost a lot of big fish because I failed to consider this phenomenon. As the distance between you and the rainbow closes, drop the rod tip. This puts the split shot below the surface, effectively stopping any pendulum action. When the steelhead runs, let it go. Then bring it back. Keep the weight below the surface, use a light drag and you'll land your prize.

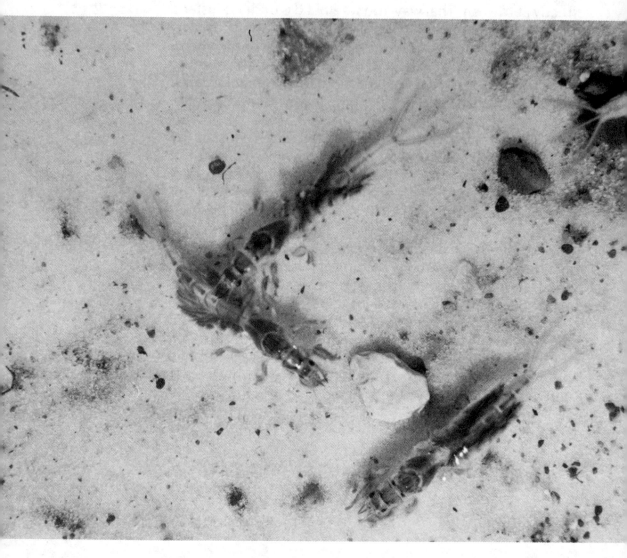

Figure 20. Wigglers or "swimming" mayfly nymphs are excellent steelhead fare both spring and fall.

CHAPTER 5
MAYFLY NYMPHS (WIGGLERS) AND METHODS FOR FISHING THEM

If there's a Magic bait for River Steelheaders, particularly those using lite-line tactics, it's the "wiggler" or mayfly nymph. Throughout the spawning season (pre, mid, and post periods) steelhead are taken on these succulent aquatic invertebrates and during low water periods they're the only bait which consistently produce strikes. When all else fails, hang a "wiggler" on a wide-bend hook and you'll take fish. Guaranteed.

Actually, the word "wiggler" is Great Lakes parlance for mayfly nymphs classified in the families *Ephemerellidae* (crawling nymphs) and *Ephemeridae* (silt-dwelling Burrowers). Both groups are active throughout their life cycles, and when swimming display a characteristic undulating body motion — thus the name "wiggler." Astute fly fisherman observed this behavioral quirk years ago and when dredging nymphs imitating *Ephemerella subvaria-Hendrickson* or *E. dorthea-Sulphur Dun*, a slight twitching

63

motion was added to the presentation. This seemingly minute twist often brought trout to creel that might otherwise shun the feathery counterfeits. Taking the mimic one step further, fly tiers have recently articulated wiggler nymphs with fine wire hinges, and the result is both immediate and deadly. I'll cover nymphing with flies in more detail during Chapter 6 — Steelheading with Flies.

It should be no surprise to river steelheaders that "wigglers" get top billing as *the* bait for catching on, for both wild and hatchery steelhead learn early that mayfly nymphs are there for the taking. In the *Ephemerellid* groups, for instance, habitat preferences (gravel, rubble, leaf drift, and detritus) put bottom-hugging fingerlings in constant contact with molting nymphs year round. The same is true with burrowing nymphs such as *Hexagenia* and *Ephemera.*

Earlier, however, it was thought these immatures seldom left their U-shaped burrows, yet in Justin and Fannie Leonard's Book, *Mayflies of Michigan Trout Streams,* they tell how trout make a living on these morsels, fall, winter and spring. Stomach autopsies showed fish fed regularly on all nymphs, so it follows that any month a steelhead is in a river, he'll avail himself to such fare, and no one knows this better than the UL trouter.

Looking at the typical life cycle of the Giant Mayfly, *Hexagenia limbata,* (over a 12 month period) shows the species undergoes more than 30 instars or molts before becoming an adult. In prime bottom habitats (3 to 6 inches of marl-based silt), according to Leonard, a square foot of stream bottom can support as many as 500 nymphs. Theoretically then, a 10 x 10 area could maintain up to 50,000 nymphs (100 sq. ft. x 500 nymphs per sq. ft.). At any one time, however, only a fraction of these molting nymphs are exposed, yet over a rivers' course, this number could rise into the hundreds of thousands. This in mind, it's safe to assume that "wigglers" are, without question, a mainstay in a trout's diet, including migrating steelhead.

Like most anglers in the east and midwest, my first exposure to "wigglers" came from outings for yellow perch. Since burrowing mayflies are common fauna in inland lakes, panfish i.e. perch, bluegills, bass, etc. utilize the nymphs year round. Ten seasons ago I was on Houghton Lake (a prime 19.5 thousand acre pond near Houghton Lake, Michigan) trying my luck on jumbo bluegills. I expected plenty of action that week, so I bought a slug of "wigglers" — 15 dozen or so — that way, I wouldn't run out. After three hours, I conceded the first round to the fish. Dejected, my first impulse was to dump the excess nymphs in the clear waters of Sand Bay, but after some thought I settled on putting them to good use on a trout stream, west of Houghton, the Little South Branch, Pere Marquette River. On past outings, this fine stream had yielded limit catches of brown trout on Ultralight spinners, so I was anxious to "Field Test" the nymphs.

My first drift in the gin-clear waters netted a plump 8 incher. Dejavu' was running on schedule as my rod danced a second time. That brown measured an even foot, and the story continued. By the time I reached the third pool, I'd landed five browns on as many nymphs. Whalla! I'd found the magic formula. Trouting would never be the same.

The second test came a week later on a trout/steelhead stream some 60 miles north, the Platte River, near Honor, Michigan. I'd flyfished the Platte earlier in April, and failed to take a steelhead. Now, however, a late spring and late run of silver fish put the river on line . . . all I need do, I thought, was show up, cast a line and land that prize rainbow. Sounded easy enough, yet for my best efforts I only hooked one fish. So, I retreated to Honor for the magic bait. At Bud's Trout Emporium, I bought another slug of "wigglers," and headed for the river.

When my wife Joan and I began drifting nymphs in a series of deep holes east of town, it was 1:00 p.m. The sun was high overhead and warm. Perfect day for sunbathing, I mused, but for steelheading? After 30 minutes I decided it was time to move upstream. Joan, however, liked the setup, so we stayed. I didn't blame her. She'd had enough of the fishing buddy routine that morning, lugging cameras and rods for more than five hours.

"Why don't you chum this hole with a handful of

"wigglers," Joan suggested. "We do it with perch when they're not looking. It might work here." Until then, I hadn't given thought to such trouting heresy, yet it was worth a try. Moments later I tossed a couple dozen nymphs into the crystalline waters and we waited. Five minutes later, I threaded two wigglers on a wide-bend Mustad, size 10.

Joan was mid-way through the second drift when her rod dipped downward. Immediately, a silver torpedo in the 4 pound class rocketed skyward, then ploughed a path downstream. I headed it off on the first bend and netted the prize. After that episode, I couldn't drag her away. Eventually she gave in, but not until she'd landed another steelhead — a twin of the first. By 3:00 we'd probed four holes, hooking five steelhead, landing one. The others, as she put it, were "potbellies" out of control.

Rigging for bottom bouncing wigglers is a simple affair and follows the guidelines set out in Chapter 3 — Bottom Bouncing. Regardless of the season, the goal is to present the nymph in the least threatening manner. The best way to accomplish this is using a fine diameter, clear mono leader, 4 to 7 feet. Remember, refinement is the key. If water conditions are normal and you're probing holding water (pools, deep runs) string a 5 foot, 4 pound-test leader. No action, drop to 2 pound-test and lengthen to 6 feet.

The philosophy behind long, fine leaders centers on the "Fear Factor." The less a steelhead is alarmed by a drifting bait, the more likely it is to "take." Long, fine leaders "search" through a rivers' strata (top to bottom) and if the offering moves through a lie in a drag-free manner, the steelhead will be attracted.

There are times, however, when short leaders are preferred, (high water and while fishing redds). Now, steelhead move little or not at all to mouth a drifting bait, so it's essential to drop the "wiggler" right on the fish's nose. A short leader simply makes the job easier.

As the season progresses and spawning fish become targets, the "wiggler" comes into its own as a "selector" bait. Steelhead holding in redd areas are not interested in

Figure 21. Joan Quinn shows sleek steelhead that inhaled drifting wiggler at mid-day on Platte River northern Michigan.

feeding, yet an intrusion into their realm (bait or fish) is immediately addressed. This situation usually occurs late in the season when water levels have stabilized or during low water. Drifting wigglers under such conditions is exacting work and calls for specific rigging.

The normal three-way swivel rig is replaced by a No. 10 Japanned barrel swivel and instead of a dropper line and split shot, .17 lead wire is wrapped around the swivel. The outfit drifts, "rolls" along irregular bottoms with ease and hangups are minimized. Not so with the three way setup. If you can't locate lead wire, one or two No. 3/0 shot pinched above the two way swivel (mainline mono) will be okay. In reduced flows, the weight of the swivel should put the wiggler on bottom.

Launching such flyweight rigs is possible by traditional casting, but I prefer to "lob" the offering into the target zone. With a 10 to 12 foot rod and an equal amount of line, you can easily cover the immediate area. Further out, strip several lengths of mono with the left hand (flyrod fashion) and feed with the index finger. I try to limit such casting to 20 feet beyond the top guide. Then, there's less chance of line fouling.

Leaders for barrel swivel setups are typically fragile (1-2-3 & 4 pound-test), so it's good practice to double loop the monofilament through each eyelet, and finish with a reverse clinch knot (same for hook). Moisten the nylon with saliva before tightening. This lubricates the mono and prevents heat buildup. I know it improves knot strength, particularly during cold weather (freezing and below).

The best presentation for wiggler rigs is slightly upstream and quartering across current, that way, the short leader (3 to 4 foot) sweeps through a lie, bait first, then weight. I find this setup/method particularly effective late in the season when several males are addressing one female.

Another technique used to drift mayfly nymphs, bait on both Great Lakes and west coast rivers employs a float similar to those used for panfishing. Tailor-made for troubled waters, i.e. eddies, slack currents below hydro dams, mid-stream pockets, holes, snag-filled bottoms, etc., bobber fishing allows an angler to probe river lies which were previously off limits to traditional bottom-bouncing setups.

West coast steelheaders have used floats for decades on a number of famous rivers in southern British Columbia, including the Campbell, Thompson and Coquihalla Rivers, but the tactic is relatively new in the midwest. During the Spring of 1968, a dedicated rainbow chaser from Farwell, Michigan, Archie Sweet and his dad Arch Sr. started floating bobbers below Tippy Dam on the Big Manistee River near Bretheran, and after two fantastic seasons on fall-run rainbows, the method caught on. Today, I doubt if you could find a lite-liner in the Great Lakes without a float in his vest. I use them throughout the season, spring, fall and winter and find them indispensable.

Rigging for float fishing follows the basic guidelines established earlier with the barrel swivel setup, but with minor changes in leader length and split shot attachment.

Knot the main line monofilament to the swivel (size 10 or 12) using a reverse clinch. Double loop the eye for strength. Do the same for your leader, but extend the mono to suit water depth. If the area probed is 5 foot, spool 3 feet, and attach a wide-bend bait hook, Size 12 or 14. Now, you're ready to attach the split shot.

The main line mono (just above the swivel) gets one or two No. 4/0s. The goal is to set the float in a vertical position. Since leader pound-test is in the 2 to 4 pound range, use removable type split shot. Why? Regular shot crimps the leader, weakening it. But with "jawed" lead, the mono isn't damaged. If you can't locate the latter, go easy with pressure. Otherwise, you'll lose the battle, long before it gets started.

Approximately 2 to 3 feet from the hook (depending on water depth) pinch a single No. 7 shot to the leader. This weight keeps the "wiggler" in the target zone (bottom), where resting steelhead can pounce on it. Remember, the shot should ride just above the bottom during the drift.

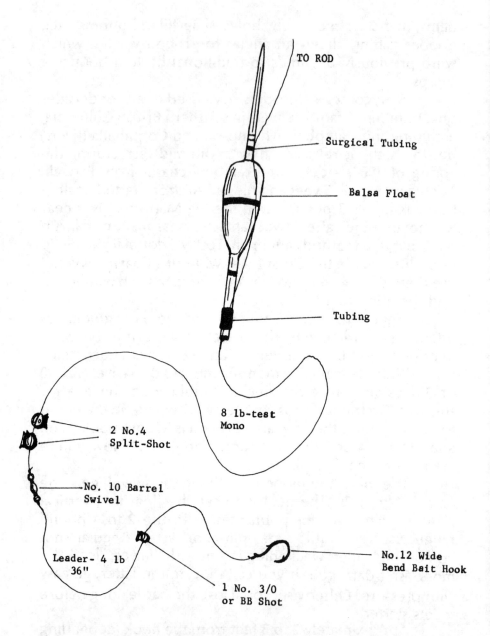

TO ROD

Surgical Tubing

Balsa Float

Tubing

8 lb-test
Mono

2 No.4
Split-Shot

No. 10 Barrel
Swivel

Leader- 4 lb
36"

1 No. 3/0
or BB Shot

No.12 Wide
Bend Bait Hook

Figure 22. Proper float rigging uses surgical tubing at line connection.
Top band avoids twisting main monofilament.

The standard bobber used in midwestern steelheading is the Carlisle No. 490, a multi-colored, balsa float made in Coldwater, Michigan. The design is perfect with one exception — line attachment. A coiled spring is used to clip the float to the monofilament and this can lead to problems: i.e. line pressure, nicked mono and lost bobbers. The solution? Replace the spring with surgical tubing, the type used to rig pencil lead to terminal setups.

First, push the spring up the shaft or remove it. Now, pull a section of rubber band into the line slot and trim both sides. This cushion protects the monofilament while fishing and through an extended battle. A one inch segment of tubing is slipped into place over the line slot and the float is ready to fish.

Depending on the depth, attach the bobber to main line mono and begin drifting. If a hangup occurs, adjust the float up or down and repeat the process. With the line resting against rubber, the task is easily accomplished.

A steelhead holding in "cover" or protected areas will simply inhale your drifting nymph, so watch the float's progress. A hesitation, side movement or dipping is your clue to "strike." By this, I mean lift the rod up and back in a single, fluid motion. No need to force it. If a steelhead is there, the line pressure will sink the barb home. From there on out, keep the rod in a tight "C" bend and if the luck is in your corner, you'll net the prize.

At times the bobber will dip under and you'll miss the steelhead. With the possible exception of yellow perch, no fish is more adept at stripping a baited hook than a rainbow. When this happens, try "hanging" the "wiggler" by or through the tough wing pads located on the mesothorax (middle body). By slipping the wide bend hook under this segment, the bait drifts naturally, plus there's a large hook gap. If this fails, "hang" two nymphs and continue drifting. Steelhead can't count and the extra action/movement could trigger an explosive take.

To get the most mileage from "wigglers," store in a container which allows free movement of oxygen. Since nymphs breathe through a series of feathery gills located on the abdomen, they should be covered by fresh water. Styrofoam bait canisters keep wigglers fit and alive for days, and are preferred. Metal wade buckets are fine, if the water is periodically changed. Otherwise, the nymph will die quickly, thus destroying their effectiveness.

CHAPTER 6
UL STEELHEADING WITH FLIES

Since I began serious pursuit of anadromous rainbows back in 1970, the dark persistent myth that steelhead are difficult to take on flies has followed me around the river circuit, midwest and west, and from what I can tell the conspiracy, although easing somewhat, continues. Most of the negativism stems from bait chuggers who insist steelhead only respond to salmon eggs or at best a plug bounced near bottom, and to go after *gairdneri* armed only with feathers and steel is not only foolhardy, but a job for the angling Elite. For these individuals, I've got news.

Actually, the handicap flies present lay not in the method, but in the delivery system. Think about it. When using standard fly tackle, the toughest problem is getting the fly on the bottom. By using Hi D tips and fast sinking lines the job can be done, but not without sacrifice. Drag on both line and leader is considerble. Accuracy and distance are also tough. If you are able to mend the drift and keep a straight line between you and the fly, fish on may follow. Yet, this is only the start of our problems.

Once the steelhead makes a sizzling run downstream, its path reverses. The looped flyline drags in the current, putting undue pressures on both hook and leader. By using a 10 foot, 10 wt. graphite rod and 12 pound-test tippet, a flyrodder can lift sufficient line from the river surface to lessen the threat, but alas, few anglers come equipped with such heavy artillery. Result, the steelhead winds his merry way downriver, free to fight again.

With the UL artist, we have a totally different picture. Instead of dragging fly lines and leaders, the lite-liner has a direct link to stream lies. By using monofilament main lines, friction — the nemesis of traditional fly tactics — is reduced or non-existent. When the three-way swivel and dropper are ticking bottom, the fly rides along at the same level, regardless of leader length. Additionally, the extended glass lifts excess line from the river surface, so there's a straight route from rod tip to fish.

As with other forms of steelheading, the name of the game with flies is to present your offering "right on the fish's nose," that way, the rainbow finds it hard to resist. Fly fishermen converting to long rods and light leaders outfish traditional salmonid anglers 10 to 1, because he enjoys the same action as a light-line (3-4 line) flyrod, but with none of its drawbacks.

By using a 10 to 12 foot rod only a short length of mono enters river currents, so the long, fine leader flows/drifts seemingly unattached. Reduced main line friction puts the fly on bottom quickly with a minimum of lead, and the "light" feeling of "finesse" fishing returns. Translated, the steelheader detects more strikes and more "Fish On" result. Landing them, however, is another story.

Earlier in Chapter 1 — Pre-Ultralight, I related the tale of my baptism into the ranks of spin-fishing with flies on the famous "Flies Only" section of the Pere Marquette River near Baldwin, Michigan, and since then, I've refined the tactic to the point where I can definitely offer frank advise to the uninitiated. Since part of my success stems directly from the P.M.s water quality and regulations, I feel the story is worth mentioning.

Like other midwestern and western steelhead rivers, the headwaters of the P.M. flow clear, clean and cold-spring and fall. In its lower reaches near Ludington, the waterway alternates between deep pools and runs, but upstream the stream's character changes. Here, the amber currents sweep over sand and gravel stretches 1 to 3 feet deep — ideal spawning water for migrating rainbows. With crystalline waters and visible targets we have the makings of a boom or bust fishery, yet for traditional flyrodders the emphasis is on bust. Why?

Most of the problem stems from the "Holy Water" practice of using "meat stick" tactics for spawning steelhead. Typically, fly flickers here string a 9 wt. line on a matching graphite and have at it. The large diameter flyline dictates using heavy-duty leaders. Strong tippets turn steelhead off, and we're back to zero. With the exception of early morning and late evening (night), flyrodders on the P.M. have a rough time of it.

Three springs ago, I put together a 9½ foot UL flyrod just for fishing the "Flies Only" water and although I've licked the problem of handling light leaders, I'm unable to lift or mend the Weight Forward 4 line properly in heavy currents, so the nemesis of dragging leaders persists. Recently, (1983 season) I substituted a 30 foot segment of number one shooting line for the standard flyline and I'm able to pull the mono clear of currents during casting and fighting, thus reducing pressures on fragile 2 and 3 pound-test leaders. Before then, I simply relied on Michigan fishing regulations to help out.

As Michigan law reads, the only tackle requirement on the flies — only stretch of the P.M. is that an artificial fly can be used, so spinning tackle is legal gear on restricted waters. Traditional flyrodders look askance at anglers toting such gear on fly water, yet many of these same individuals carry a spare spool loaded with straight monofilament — just in case.

Actually, a fly reel loaded with monofilament is all

that's needed to reach steelhead on most waters. With the exception of the largest of midwest and west coast rivers, there's little need to lay out a long cast to put your fly in front of resting fish. By adding split shot to terminal setups, a short lob cast accomplishes the goal nicely, particularly when fishing redd areas. If distance is needed, a roll cast similar to the British Spey method is best. Master the techniques and you'll cover the water.

Since flyfishing is best conducted during mid and late season, the angler should concentrate his efforts here. In headwater gravels, the tactic is Sight Fishing to visible targets, so the steelheader can concentrate on technique rather than finding fish. Sounds easy enough, but there are problems.

To many anglers, steelhead remain a mystery fish which shows spring and fall, and the circumstances surrounding its arrival and departure remain an enigma. As I related in Chapter 3 — Bottom Bouncing — the average trouter locates rainbows by following the crowd. The practice finds favor among amateurs, but it leaves dedicated fishermen cold. For them, facts are the only way.

Timing. If there's a key to successful steelheading with flies, this is it. Since migrations are initiated/triggered by water temperatures the angler should follow them closely — no easy task. From year to year, season to season, spring and fall the magic temperature changes (42-45 d. F), and the push into headwaters can be delayed as much as a week or two either way. A late winter, for instance, keeps estuaries cold and steelhead seek warmer temperatures lakeward. An early spring accompanied by warm rains raise river temperatures and the push into headwaters is on.

Initially, schools of silver fish swarm at rivermouths and after a few false starts, they head swiftly upstream, with brief rest stops along the way. Fishery biologists follow these migrations closely and are good sources of "where to" and "when to" information. Ned Fogle, Anadromous Specialist with Michigan's Department of Natural Resources indicates migrating rainbows travel from 2.5 to 4 miles per day. By

Figure 23. Heavyweight steelhead are taken on flies using UL rods, spin and fly. A smooth drag is the key.

using these figures, it's a simple task to estimate the prime arrival time in spawning headwaters.

One of my favorite steelhead rivers in southwestern Michigan is the Rogue River, a tributary to the Grand River, some 12 miles north of Grand Rapids. From the Grand's mouth at Grand Haven, to Rockford, (Rogue's headwaters) the distance is 32 miles + or -. Divide this figure by 2.5 or 4 and we come up with 12.8 and 8 respectively. In other words somewhere between 8 and 12 days from the time steelhead enter rivermouth regions, one can expect fish to show in spawning headwaters. Over the years/seasons I've found the system to be accurate (usually on the plus side by 1 or 2 days). I know it sure beats running to the river for periodic temperature checks.

When I began serious steelheading back in the early 70's, I relied totally on local contacts (tackle shops, charter captains, etc.) to track migrating fish, but these sources were unreliable. Now, I simply call the DNR Regional Post nearest the river I want to hit for up to the minute reports (phone numbers are listed in current Fishing Guide, Orders). When rainbows are being taken in rivermouths, mark the calendar, measure the distance to spawning waters and show up on time. And, don't ignore trouters/steelheaders in your home town. Trout Unlimited and Steelhead Chapters are natural grapevines of early breaking information/hotspots and a membership in either organization can pay big dividends, not only in fish on, but also as a voice investment in the sport's future.

As migrations continue, steelhead use traditional runs, glides and holding waters until spawning gravels are reached upstream. The key to taking fish now is knowing the location of these set paths and repeated drifts on bottom. But, alas, such is not the case. Most anglers bounce their offering five to ten times, declare the lie fishless and move on. Successful early season steelheading, fly or bait requires the trouter work every foot of the stream bottom. Resting rainbows will not move to mouth a fly, so you must hit the fish right on the nose.

During mid-season, steelhead numbers increase significantly, as does competition for spawning gravel. The higher water temperatures further catalyze aggressive behavior and for fly anglers drifting suggestive patterns like Spring Nymphs, Atherton Squirrel Tails or Carrie Specials, some exciting fly action can be had, but remember, it's color more than pattern that's important, so stock your vest with a variety of hues including red, pink, orange, yellow, chartreuse, black and brown, Size 6, 2 x long.

Rigging for early and mid-season follows bottom-bouncing guidelines: three-way swivel, dropper and trailing leader, 4 to 5 foot, 4 pound-test. I like to tick bottom constantly, then I can "walk" the fly to resting steelhead. When the rig hangs up, lift the rod tip and the current should sweep the fly over new territory. If not, adjust split shot numbers until the goal is achieved, and work at it.

Once steelhead reach spawning gravel, our strategy switches from "blind" to "visual" fishing. In crystalline headwaters, females pound out a series of redds and deposit from 500 to 1200 eggs, which are, in turn, fertilized by a single dominate male. Early on, flies mimicking spawn clusters and single eggs are very effective, particularly when fished with a three-way swivel setup, on a short leader, 3½ to 4 feet, 4 pound-test.

One of my favorites is a pattern dubbed Two Egg Sperm Fly, Size 8, 2 x long. The body consists of two chenille "eggs" separated by a band of fine gold tensile and a shelled back of either fluorescent calf tail or molon yarn. Depending on water clarity and light level, I tie the fly in a variety of colors, including chartreuse, pink, orange, or dark cerise (red). In early morning and clear water use chartreuse or orange with a white back. As the day wears on, switch to hot pink or red. If one color combo doesn't pay off, experiment.

Four seasons ago, my wife Joan (my favorite fishing buddy) and I were probing a series of redds on the Muskegon River downstream from Newaygo, Michigan. It was April 23rd and despite the fact that we had steelhead porpoising all around us, we failed to hook a fish. From 6:30

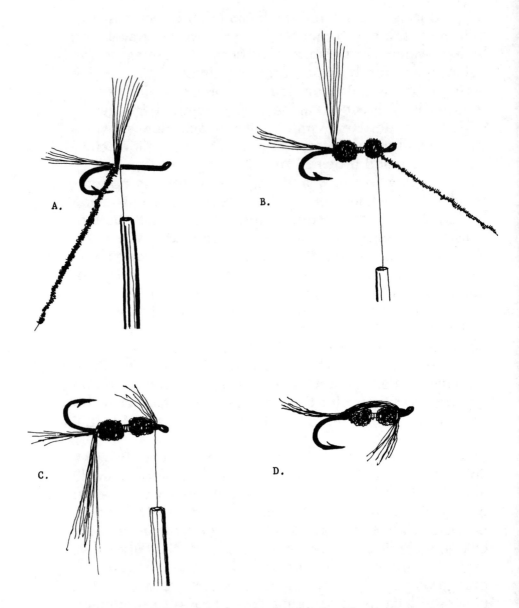

Figure 24.   Tying procedure for Double Egg Fly. Use hot colors in early morning-dark at mid-day.

to 9 o'clock we drifted nymphs, yarn flies and sperm sac flies, but drew a blank. At 10 o'clock the river level dropped drastically, and the already tough conditions became critical.

Through my polaroids I spotted several steelhead finning in the thin water, so I tied on a hot orange, single egg fly, Size 12, gold tag, with a sparse wing of red maribou. On the second drift (much to my surprise), a crimson-sided male nailed the bit of chenille. Ten minutes later, I was fast to another silver bullet in the 5 pound class. At noon the action ended, but by then Joan and I hooked three fish each, landing a total of 4. The magic formula, 2 pound-test leaders 4 feet long and single egg flies. Since that time, a segment of my flybox is devoted entirely to chenille egg flies in various colors, and over the last three springs, they've become our ace-in-the-hole.

Rigging for critical/shallow waters consists of a Size 10 or 12 barrel swivel knotted into the main line monofilament. For weight, pinch two BB split shot on the heavy mono or cover the swivel with a single layer of .17 lead wire. The leader is double looped and finished with a reverse clinch or palomar knot. Double loop the hook also, and the fragile leader will hold through an extended battle.

The tactic here is to keep a direct link between you and the drifting egg fly. Approach the holding fish from downstream, lob-cast the offering above the target, keeping the rod tip high. When the line stops, hesitates or moves sideways, strike. With polaroids it's tough or impossible to see the "take," so watch the line where it enters the water.

During mid season, spring rains often swell river currents to flood levels and water clarity drops sharply. Turbulent conditions are tailor-made for baits/lures such as spawn bags, spin and wobble glos or plugs, yet a simple yarn fly produces just as well, if it's worked on bottom.

Two falls ago, while drifting the Center Run, Grand River, 6th Street Dam, Grand Rapids, Michigan, I limited out on salmonids using chartreuse yarn snelled to a No. 42 Wide Bend Eagle Claw. A heavy thunderstorm on October 10th put the river 2 feet above normal and dirty. Wade fishing was impossible, so I launched a 10 foot pram, motored into position and went to work. Once I got the offering on bottom I took steelhead, coho, browns and kings — all fell for the fluff of poly yarn.

The best part about fishing these flies is cost. A single hook, a few strands of yarn and you're in business. Most steelhead rivers are snag-filled and losing terminal rigs is part of the story. By using yarn flies the bite on the wallet is eased, and there's no need to buy spawn clusters. If the rainbows aren't attracted, scent the fly in cod liver oil and hang on.

By late April or early May, most steelhead have spawned and turned homeward (lake or ocean), but the fishing is far from over. By walking the river and searching carefully with polaroids the enterprising trouter can always locate a few late arrivals. Quite often, these singular females are surrounded by a number of surplus males, thus the stage is set for some spectacular fly fishing . . . *if* the trouter matches his techniques to late season conditions.

Actually, post-season periods are more suited to fly than bait fishing, for a number of reasons. In late April or early May, river levels have stabilized and currents flow, clear and low. With fewer females pounding gravel, surplus eggs are not as numerous, and steelhead are immediately suspicious of spawn clusters flowing in crystalline waters. By using mini clusters (6 steelhead or 3 salmon eggs) in early morning, it's possible to take fish, yet more often than not, standard bait setups force rainbows to flee. Drift a fly and we have a different ball game altogether.

Put yourself in the fish's place. It's early May and the river is running low and clear. Water depth is 3 feet and every pebble is in full view. Now, enter a drifting bait, leader and swivel rig. If the lure doesn't frighten the steelhead, his trailing swivel and split shot will. Wham! The fish sulks or spooks, and we're back to zero.

By running flies, the steelheader lessens the threat factor considerably. There's no three-way swivel. The weight, however slight, is located well away from the resting

Figure 25. Fly fishing is tailor-made for shallow water, late season steelhead. Fish are not frightened by drifting flies.

fish. The drifting fly is a natural part of a streams' environs, and the steelhead is instinctively attracted. Earlier in Chapter 3, I mentioned how young steelhead learn early to recognize nymphs as food and feed on the invertebrates year round. When the smolts return as adults 3 years later, this innate feeding pattern is still intact.

Since 90% of late season steelheading is working visible targets, the angler must "finesse" each hookup. Poor presentation and careless wading will only get you into trouble. With the early season crowd pursuing other interests, the flyfisher literally has the river to himself, so the pace is slow, deliberate. Reduced pressures permit the steelheader to concentrate on strategy, rather than on "grab the fish and run!" Once spawning fish are located, the "selective" plan goes into high gear.

With the female serving as the center of all spawning activity, we must avoid hooking her and concentrate on the addressing males lying below her. If the female is accompanied by a single male, work only on this fish. Hook the female, and all spawning activity will end. Hook the male, however, and he will soon be replaced by a subordinate male . . . the spawning continues and we have another target to work on!

The casting pattern should be upstream and behind the female. Adjust weight and leader length until the goal is achieved. I usually start with a 4 to 5 foot leader, 2 pound-test knotted to a No. 10 Japanned barrel swivel. The weight of the swivel should put the fly in the target zone. If not, add a few wraps of lead wire or a single BB shot on the main line mono.

By using the lob cast, targets within 20 to 30 feet can easily be reached. Accuracy is important, so concentrate on putting the fly below the female. No action, lengthen the leader a foot and continue drifting. Reducing fly size might also help. I begin with 6s and drop to 8s or 10s in critical waters. It's doubtful you could fish a fly so small a steelhead couldn't see it, but there are practical considerations. Hook gap and wire size are important to hooking and holding that prize rainbow, and smaller sizes don't give any margin for error.

Although there are a number of fly patterns which produce consistently during late season, I tend to favor suggestive patterns like the Spring Nymph created by Ron Spring, Muskegon, Michigan. Tied in a variety of sizes (6, 8, & 10s) and body colors on Mustads No. 9671, the steelheader will be able to cover all situations.

Another productive pattern that's received a lot of attention lately is the stonefly nymph tied on Mustads No. 36890, Size 8 and 10. As females pound headwater gravel, nymphs in the *plecopteran* group, both *Taeniopteryx* and *Pteronarcys*, are dislodged and steelhead, male and female, pick up these freebees. Why they do this is open to speculation, but it no doubt centers on feeding behavior acquired during the smolt stage.

One more possible reason relates to the male steelheads aggressive behavior during spawning. Once paired with a female, the male "protects" the redd area from any and all intrusions — steelhead or fly. Repeated drifts through a nest area are territorial threats and the dominate male moves swiftly to end the invasion, mouthing the bait repeatedly. From past experience, I know this assessment is accurate, for within minutes after placing a stonefly in front of an addressing male, he's solidly hooked.

Streamer flies are also classed as antagonistic patterns and have large audiences both in the Great Lakes and west coast. The tactic, as with stoneflies, is essentially the same; tease the male into striking. It's tough, however, to repeatedly put the bulky flies in front of spawning steelhead without spooking them. Using a three-way swivel setup and short leader the goal can be achieved, but the rig should be fished early or late, during low light levels.

The lob cast is the most efficient way to handle streamers. I generally run a 3 foot section of 4 pound-test mono, knotted to the swivel and 2, No. 7 shot pinched to the dropper. By adjusting our casting pattern, from behind, we can fish to the males only.

My favorite pattern is a white Mylar Maribou, Size 6, 4 x long. Another productive fly is a blue and white bucktail, silver body, tied sparse. In a contest, the maribou pattern easily wins because the pulsating wing seems alive, prodding the steelhead into action. It may take 50 or more casts, but stick with it. No maribou streamer on hand? Tie on a colorful standard feather wing pattern like the Royal Coachman or Alaska Mary Ann. I think accuracy is more important than menu, so put the fly on target.

Again, the casting strategy (streamer or nymph) is to the male only. Hook the female and you'll have to find a new location. Even though the female isn't feeding, she may pick up the drifting fly, but the male will do it repeatedly.

The take will not be overt, so watch the mono closely. When it hesitates, lift the rod. Once the fish is on, lower the glass. This gets the rainbow's head below the surface (where it belongs). Most anglers, however, reef on the rod and either pull the hook or straighten it out. Once the steelhead is under control, reapply butt pressure.

Periodically you'll find an active redd with a single female, a dominate male and a lineup of addressing subordinates. Here, the tactic is males only, but we must direct our fly to the last fish in the formation. By hooking the rear fish and backing it down, it's possible to pick off every male in the redd, without disturbing the female. Sounds pretty tough, but by adjusting the drift, up or downstream, you can place the fly in front of the trailing fish.

Last season (1984) I came across a situation similar to the one just described and in the hour and a half that followed (12 to 1:30) I hooked eight males, landing 3. The fly was a Dun-Gray Stonefly, Size 8. When the action died, I rested the redd until 3 p.m. By then, a number of surplus males had located the female and the program continued. This time, however, male reorganization was undisciplined, with subordinates darting everywhere. To catch one, I simply drifted the fly anywhere behind the female and Wham, "Fish On!"

CHAPTER 7
BOBBER FISHING STEELHEAD

If anyone a decade ago had told me there were groups of steelheaders, west and midwest, who use bobbers, long rods and light leaders to take limit catches of *anadromous* rainbows, I wouldn't have believed it. Yet af eight full seasons of river-hopping along steelhead by-v in both U.S. and Canada, I'm a firm believer. The technique works as well as any system I've tried on steelies — spring, fall or winter.

Actually, the tactic of using bobbers to buoy baits is a Canadian invention, and from research it appears the method has been in use for years on a number of southern British Columbia rivers including the Campbell, Thompson and Coquihalla. Guides here developed the system to hold baits off rough, snag-filled bottoms, and somewhere along the line, bobber fishing migrated south to Washington, Oregon and California. From there, the method found it's way into midwestern steelhead streams and today, it's so firmly entrenched, I doubt one could find a dedicated rainbow chaser without a float or two tucked into his vest. All I can say is "welcome!"

The tale behind bobbers for Great Lakes' steelhead is an interesting one and dates back a dozen years or so. At the time Archie Sweet, a noted Michigan steelheader from Farwell, MI., and his father Archie, Sr., were searching for a technique that would permit fishing slack waters below Tippy Dam. They knew steelhead were there most of the year, but traditional bottom-bouncing methods didn't work. The slow current created drag and the fish were wise to their best efforts.

At first, the obvious solution of floating baits with bobbers escaped their brainstorming sessions. Then it hit them. On numerous occasions they'd encountered perch fishermen at Tippy with steelhead on their stringers. Was their success a fluke or would a rainbow consistently strike a buoyant bait? The logical way to find out was through field testing, not just on the Manistee, but on other difficult waters.

During Spring 1968 and into winter, Sweet and another steelheader, Larry Sivak, put the float to work. Laboring under the theory that a bobber would function best on slack waters, their first efforts were directed at rivers controlled by hydro dams.

From there the anglers hit traditional runs, slicks and holding waters on many of the famous rivers draining both coasts, east and west/Huron and Michigan, the Au Sable, Au Gres, Betsie, Platte, Little Manistee, Big Manistee and Pere Marquette. Their findings were universal and sensational!

Limit catches on steelhead became routine for both men. Waters that were previously unproductive gave up a mother lode of bright fish. For both men, "it seemed too simple." Sweet recalled the axiom "there's no easy steelhead," yet he and Sivak had to agree, "bobber fishing is a very consistent method of taking rainbows, if you believe in the technique and stick with it."

Every season, I run into anglers who think bobber fishing is the solution to all their steelheading problems. Far from it. Steelheading is steelheading regardless of the method involved. The principles of finding and probing productive waters still apply in bobber fishing. The float, however, keeps the average guy out of bottom trouble and his bait in front of fish.

Apart from the visual clue of a strike, bobber fishing offers an angler a number of advantages, none of which can be approached by traditional bottom techniques. Each can and often does make the difference in fish hooked.

Perhaps the biggest advantage with this style of angling is the freedom steelheaders have in probing snag-filled pools and runs, dead water, mid-stream pockets, etc. Even though many parts of a river hold fish, getting your offering to them is tough, if not impossible. Potentially productive waters are often passed up because they're unapproachable. But with the float, you're halfway home.

My first experience with bobber fishing was steelheading at its best. Everything I and my wife Joan touched that early December day turned to silver and we weren't alone.

The location was a seamless stretch of water below Tippy Dam on the Big Minstee River, east of Brethern, MI. After a full week of Indian Summer the big rainbows were on the move again and the coffer dam below the main impoundment was stacked with silver fish. Although the thermometer registered a frigid 11 degrees at daybreak, the fishing was red-hot.

In two days of intensive angling, our group of ten fishermen strung 75 steelhead for an average of 3.5 fish per day. Exceptional fishing you say? I agree, but the entire story isn't revealed until one analyzes the techniques used to take the fish. Out of the total, only 6 rainbows were taken by traditional bottom-bouncing, the remainder fell to bobber fishing! Why? The problem centered on the slack water below the dam.

With normal terminal rigging (three way swivel, dropper and leader) the steelheader could only drift the upper reaches of any of the runs below Tippy. Here, current tongues were strong enough to carry the bait along, but

Figure 26. Slack water below hydro-dams provide action for early winter steelheaders. Bobbers keep drifts snag-free.

when waters eddied, the offering stalled. The fish, if they were present, became wise immediately.

If you've been around dam sites you know what I'm talking about. Yet to the uninitiated, solving the problem meant lightening the dropper weight and continued drifting. That's what occurred with the bottom-bouncing anglers at Tippy, and it was this hard-nosed attitude that put fewer fish on their stringers. On the third day the die-hards caved in, but by then the action was over. A lesson to the wise.

In the tailrace section of a dam site (or any river having strong, center currents) steelhead rest and feed, not in the main current, but in edge waters created by the backwash. This cushion, depending on flume speed, can be a considerable distance, and in the case below Tippy Dam, drift lines operate for as much as 30 to 40 yards! But only for those anglers floating bobbers.

Take the story 300 to 400 yards downstream and we have another problem. Here, the river's speed increases ten-fold. Instead of contending with dead water, fishermen must slow his offering to attract steelhead. Again, traditional bottom-bouncing tactics don't work, simply because the bait zooms through the lie so quickly the trout has little time to jump on it. Yet, by using a float, the angler can stall the drift long enough to catch on.

As we continue further downriver more difficult waters emerge, but they're only problems for traditional tactics. With a float it's a different ball game. As the Manistee deepens into a wide, long run, the flow decreases appreciably and the steelheader is confronted with dragging baits, stalled drifts, plus a nightmarish jumble of logs and snags. Many anglers refuse to probe such holes and runs, but that's where the fish are. If you're going to catch on, you'll have to go in after them.

In Chapter 5 — Wigglers, 1 covered how to properly rig a bobber for drifting nymphs. It's important to follow the directions to the letter. Otherwise, you'll have trouble with snags, lost floats and the assorted headaches associated with cold weather angling, i.e. numb fingers, aching back, cold feet and spicy expletives!

To get the bobber tactic down pat, I'll walk you through the examples given above, then you'll be able to apply the technique to your own, unique situation. Of course, it's taken for granted that the fisherman has timed his arrival to coincide with the steelhead run, then the problem is one of fishing properly and not finding fish. Yes, it is true that some steelhead can be caught at any time the fish are in the river, but why hinder your best efforts. Be on hand at the peak of migration and you'll be assured of success.

In the tailrace section, begin probing edge currents, then as the float passes your position spill line. Open the bail, lift the rod tip and extend the drift into the end of the run. Control line feed with the forefinger and you'll be ready to strike instantly.

No takers, direct the next cast further downstream and continue the probe. I use a quartering upstream cast so the nymphs or spawn is on-bottom when the bobber floats by at right angles. If the float drags in the current adjust up or down and continue drifting. The goal is a smooth flow through suspected target zones.

Standard rods for bobber fishing are outsized when compared with normal UL gear. My favorite is a 12 foot stick built from an S-Glass blank by Lamiglas. The rod is light, delicate and designated for 2 to 4 pound-test leaders. The extended length allows me to lift all main line monofilament from river currents, so there's little or no drag on the drifting float. Plus, the rod permits handling fixed bobber depths and long leaders. Both advantages help extend drift lines and present a more direct hooking route.

Once edge currents are thoroughly covered, concentrate on the backwash or eddy. Here, steelhead line up with their noses tucked into current lines and a slow-moving, drag-free nymph or egg cluster fools them consistently. Keep the main line mono completely out of the water and the bobber will find its way. When the float passes your position, spill line. Work the inside and outside of the slack water until you're satisfied the area has been blanketed. No action? Take the program into mid-stream pockets further downstream.

In many steelhead waters in the midwest and west, there are deep, holding pockets in mid-river and most, if not all are tough to probe. Using traditional bottom-bouncing rigs baits sweep through these positions so quickly that resting steelhead refuse to budge. One of my favorite northwestern Michigan rivers, the Little Manistee has a number of these lies and without floating a bobber, hooking and landing a fish here is a Herculean feat akin to scaling a 1000 foot rock wall with bare hands!

The first time I took my wife Joan to the river six years ago, I thought she'd loose her split shot before she hooked a fish. First it was the snags. Then the steelhead began loading up mid-stream pockets, and if this weren't enough, a freezing rain hit the river.

When I found her below a cascading rapids near the DNR weir at Stronach she was digging in her vest looking for a bobber, to "end this pleasant misery." I rigged the colorful float and my pouting companion went to work. On the third drift through a snag-filled hole the bobber dipped. Joan responded and her 11 foot Steelheader rod danced a lively beat. Within minutes she screamed, "get the net." We exchanged glances and a baleful look washed her face. I knew I'd have to do something and fast. My net was hanging on a tree some 50 yards downstream.

In seconds I was below the wallowing steelhead and Joan slowly pumped the rod tip, urging the fish upstream. Tailing the beast was impossible, so I did the next best thing, scooped the rainbow in my arms and waded ashore. Somehow the writhing, crimson-sided male bounced just right and my protesting wife had her prize.

After that soul-wrenching episode my partner calmed down and before the action ended at 9:30, she'd hooked five steelhead, but the gilly (me) was only able to put the net on one more fish, a female in the 10 pound class. I was redeemed.

Successful probing of mid-stream pockets is possible because floats permit an angler to slow the drift long enough for a steelhead to react. Cast the bobber well above or to either side of the lie and when the cork reaches the target zone, lift the rod tip high overhead. The surface disturbance will hold the bait momentarily in place, and that's all you need. Adjust float depth until the pocket is covered, smoothly and completely.

In the deep, wide, long runs further downstream, migrating silvers rest before they continue their journey. During pre-season periods anglers probe these waters repeatedly, yet few hook fish. Again, dragging leaders are the problem. Bobbers solve the dilemma nicely because the cork presents the bait just off bottom and it drifts at river speeds. I generally work these current threads from upstream, lobbing the bobber nearby and as the float moves downstream I guide and spill line. The tactic is very similar to the drop back method used by riverboat drifters, but relies on the bobber instead of currents to transport our bait to waiting steelhead. Keep as much line from the water surface as possible throughout the probe and you'll have a straight line between you and Fish On.

During mid-season periods when visual targets are the rule, bobber fishing is very productive, if the angler probes nearby cover, i.e. brushy banks, log jams or deep river bends. When redd areas are vacant the serious steelheader knows spawning rainbows have moved to protective coverts downstream. Rig the bobber in the usual manner and knot a section of 4 pound-test to the barrel swivel, long enough to cover the bottom. Between the jawed split shot and hook there should be 2 to 3 feet of leader. This will get you in the target zone.

The drift is controlled with the rod. Lob the float next to the barrier and as it works along the jam, etc., watch the bobber closely. If it hesitates, bounces or jerks, strike immediately. Bobbers and covers work so well together because the bait is delivered along the entire length of the structure. The float works on the edge, while the bait is

Figure 27. Balsa floats make steelhead easy targets in mid-stream pockets. This silver torpedo came from troubled waters on Little Manistee River.

swept under the jam or bank where steelhead are resting. Wham! You're in business.

Another area where bobber fishing has become extremely popular is rivermouth regions, particularly on midwestern streams. Here, in both spring and fall, migrating steelhead load up, but presenting a bait to them is tough. Again, slack current is the culprit.

Near the town of Honor, Michigan, the Platte River is a steelheaders haven — clear, swift and cold, but in its lower stretches water speed is slack, so slow that drifting a bait here is virtually impossible using traditional methods. Some steelheaders have solved the problem by buoying their baits with bits of styrofoam or Korky floats. The tactic works, yet the bait stays in a limited area. Not so when floating a bobber.

During the fall of 1977, I was at the mouth of the Platte River on Lake Michigan, near Platte Point to sample the returning steelhead and even though there were hordes of rainbows below the migrating coho, I couldn't catch on. I'd tried everything — nuggets, nymphs, spawn bags, etc. I was just about to hang it up when the notion hit me, why not float a bobber in the lake!

When I began working a gray trough near the mouth, dawn was still a hint of pink on the eastern horizon. In the dim light the chartreuse and white float bobbed, weaved and drifted freely. Under the bit of cork a fresh skein of coho eggs hung enticingly. A moderate off-shore breeze helped the river currents spread the message, "over here." On the third or fourth line spill the bobber rocketed under. Seconds later a sleek-bodied steelhead launched skyward. Until I felt the surge on my line the rainbow appeared free, then with terrifying speed the fish dispelled that thought. The monofilament quickly melted from the closed-face reel as the rainbow made a wide, sweeping turn and raced shoreward. The fish shook its head furiously above the calm surface and dropped back into the lake. A quick run to the right, again a cascading leap. Ten minutes and the female steelhead came gasping on its side. In one sweeping motion I spanned the broad head and lifted the fish above the clear water.

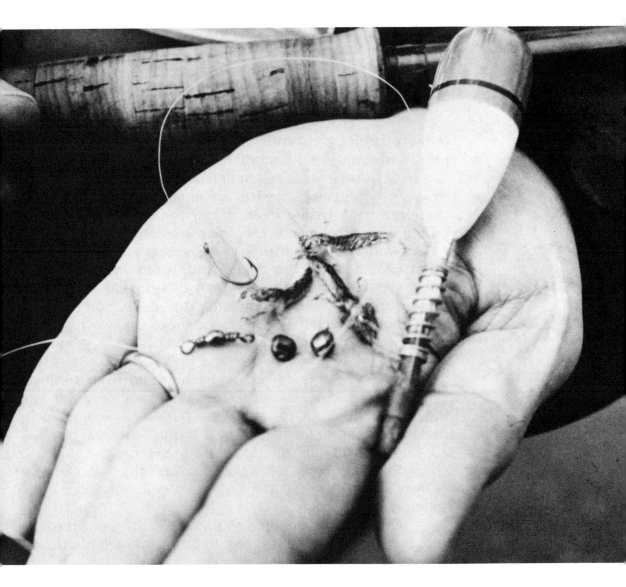

Figure 28.   Mayfly nymphs dubbed "wigglers" are THE bait on midwest rivers. Keep fresh for best results.

And so the action continued. At 7:30 a.m., however, light levels rose sharply and the fish moved lakeward. Yet in that brief period, I strung two more steelhead in the 7 pound class and added a new wrinkle in my steelheading cloth. I've also used this same technique on early-run cohos and the results are, in a word, unbelievable.

Baits for bobber fishing vary with both angler and locale. West coast and British Columbia steelheaders, for instance, prefer ghost shrimp fished live (no easy task) fresh prawns (shrimp-like decapods) or salmon/steelhead eggs, in sacs or skeins. Great Lakes anglers are partial to large burrowing mayfly nymphs like *Hexagenia limbata* (wigglers), yet many use fresh spawn to catch on. The key to successful fishing with either bait is keeping the offering fresh!

With nymphs or shrimp a steady supply of oxygenated water will keep the bait lively. And, when you hook the tidbit, slip the barb under the exoskeleton (near the head-thorax) avoiding the delicate internal parts. Some west coast anglers attach their baits to the shook shank using fine copper wire. I think is going a bit far, but if it works, who's to argue.

If you're able to secure fresh spawn from freshly caught steelhead or salmon, the egg skeins will keep well in the refrigerator, but for extended periods I recommend preserving. The following formula is quick and the results are both colorful and tough. Here's the recipe.

Start by mixing 1 cup salt (pickling salt), 1 cup borax (20 Mule Team), and 1 cup sugar. Blend well. Now place this solution in a gallon glass jar.

Cut the egg skeins into chunks. Drop these into the jar and leave for 10 minutes. Stir to keep ingredients from settling. Time this procedure!

Remove the eggs and drain. Spread on paper toweling and sprinkle with borax. Wrap the chunks in towels and store in refrigerator overnight. Finally, place eggs in tightly sealed jars. This recipe should supply you with enough eggs until steelhead return in early fall-winter, spring when you can renew your larder.

CHAPTER 8
RIGGING METHODS AND EXPERIENCES

There's no easy steelhead. Guides know it. Bait chuggers contemplate it and flyrodders philosophize it, yet each season, spring and fall, thousands of hopefuls hit the creeks, streams and rivers across the U.S. in search of the mighty *anadromous* rainbow, but few come away successful. Unless the angler is extremely lucky; hits the peak of the run or adverse weather keeps fishing pressure down, you can expect to work hard for every steelhead you land. I know several steelheaders who are going on five years and have yet to hang a fish.

As related in Chapter 1, most of my early steelheading efforts went unrewarded simply because I refused to alter the method. When I switched from fly to spin tackle my percentage of hooked fish went up, yet it wasn't until I refined the presentation and terminal rig that I felt proficient in the sport.

Quiz ten consistently successful steelheaders on their

favorite honey hole and you'll get ten different answers, but quiz them on favorite method and you'll get a unanimous voice — drift fishing. Long ago the experts recognized the importance of putting their offering on bottom. "It's not so much what you show them that matters, but how you show um." These words of wisdom come from a relative youngster in the steelheader ranks, Brian Alber, Grand Rapids, Michigan. Brian's been at the game for more than a decade now, yet he's only 22. To date, Alber's won nearly every fishing prize/contest the City Fathers and Michigan Steelheaders Association Chapter has sponsored in the Furniture City, including chinook salmon, brown trout, and recently a record laker and steelhead.

When I first met the "fishing machine" he was fifteen years old, but he was advanced enough to point out the error of my ways. It was late October and the fall migration of silver bullets was underway. Literally hundreds of big rainbows were pulled from the turbulent waters below the Grand River's 6th St. Dam Site, downtown Grand Rapids, yet I hadn't fared so well. In two long mornings of drifting I managed two lakers and one silver coho, but no steelhead.

"These fish have their noses on bottom and when they're not hiding behind a rock, they're moving across the face of the dam." Brian's voice came loud and firm above the tumbling currents. "Shorten that leader and put enough lead to get down, otherwise, you're wasting time. That long leader you're running now just rides up and the steelies don't even see the bait."

I quickly nipped off two feet of mono, knotted the hook and continued probing the boiling waters. Ten minutes later my rod throbbed wildly as a silver steelhead catapulted skyward. I turned the fish twice, but finally moved downstream. Below, my slender glass dictated the end. I released the sleek female and went back to work. By 11 o'clock my shortened tippet and skein spawn accounted for three more steelhead. Tops was a broad-bodied male in the 10 pound class.

Under normal circumstances, bait fishing is finesse fishing, particularly when dealing with spring/spawning

Figure 29. Brian Alber, top-flight steelheader from Grand Rapids Mich. lands spring fish from 6th St. Dam Site on Grand River. Spawn bag on bottom did the trick.

steelhead or when probing dam sites. At the 6th Street location long leaders are ineffective, because turbulent, undertow currents force the leader back onto the main line monofilament, fouling the drift. Or, it rides upward, out of the target zone. Fortunately water clarity on the Grand permits anglers to run 4 and 6 pound-test, and still take fish. But when currents are clear and steelhead spawning it's a different story.

When probing/drifting redd areas, long, light leaders are standard. Five, six and seven foot lengths put split shot well away from resting fish. With reduced fear factors, you at least stand a chance.

If you're working relatively snag-free bottoms the 3 way swivel rig described in Chapter 4 is ideal. There's also a similar setup using a barrel swivel in place of the three way. Knot the running monofilament to one eye and instead of trimming excess material use it as a drop line. Pinch the split shot on the surplus and you're in business. I use this setup to speed the rigging process. Since the drop mono is the same poundage as your main line, do not place a knot at the end. Then, if a hang up occurs, the shot easily slips off.

This style rig quickly converts into a bobber fishing setup, so when the need arises you're ready in seconds. At the 6th Street Site, for instance, steelhead often drop downstream into deep holding waters when angling pressures increase at the dam face. Fishing the "Quarry Pool" is tough because currents there are slow and deep, yet for the bobber toting steelheader probing the lie is a breeze. Just clip a float to your line and start drifting.

Another setup that gets a lot of attention in the Great Lakes and to some extent on the west coast is a take off on the bait walker rig used by walleye anglers. The unit consists of a three-way swivel and a pencil sinker. The lead segment is loosely wired to one eyelet. As the setup drifts downstream the sinker adjusts to bottom irregularities, thus fewer hang ups. I use the rig when rivers are high and getting on bottom requires a lot of weight.

A modified version of the 3 way-swivel rig uses a section of surgical tubing as a drop line or sinker holder. A

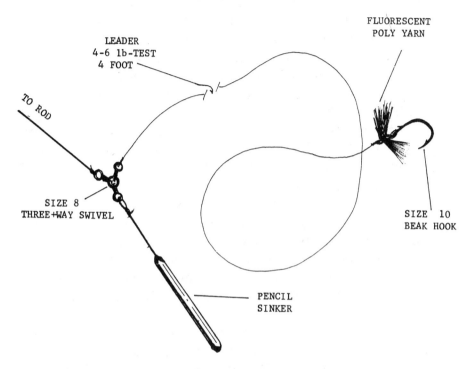

LEADER
4-6 lb-TEST
4 FOOT

TO ROD

SIZE 8
THREE-WAY SWIVEL

FLUORESCENT
POLY YARN

SIZE 10
BEAK HOOK

PENCIL
SINKER

Figure 30.   Pencil sinker rig is ideal for getting on bottom during high water. It's snag resistant and doesn't interfer with bait action.

piece of lead wire is inserted into the tubing. When snagged, the lead pulls out, freeing the rig. I use a refined version of this setup when all else fails. West coast anglers use this rig extensively, but in the Great Lakes it hasn't quite caught on.

Swivel, drop weight and leader considered, let's turn our attention to an important, but often neglected subject — knots. It's surprising how much money, time, and energy people devote to steelheading and ignore the basic link holding the whole thing together. With traditional weight monofilaments (6-8 and 10 pound-test) just about any proven knot will do, but when dealing with leaders in the 1, 2, 3 and 4 lb range special attention should be given to all connections, particularly hook knots.

Paul Johnson, Information Specialist with Berkley & Co., Trilene University, conducts seminars regularly on the subject and offers this advice. "With light, hard-finish monos (1-2 & 4 lb-test) we recommend double looping the line before finishing the knot. This creates a substantial base for the polymer to work against, particularly during extended battles."

Johnson also recommends lubricating the line with saliva before cinching. "Believe it or not heat is generated as the knot is tightened. Wetting reduces this build-up and prevents surface abrasion from occurring. Both must be reduced to gain full line efficiency."

From personal experience I can vouch for Paul's observations, particularly during cold weather. I never gave it much thought until I fished Tippy Dam seven years ago. It was December 8th, and despite the frigid 17 degree air temperature the coffer spillway below Tippy was loaded with silver fish. I, along with four other steelheaders from Clare, Midland and Saginaw were having a ball, but I was the only one losing fish. I went through three rainbows before Jake Ribicki suggested a different knot. I thought the ring-eye, wide bend Eagle Claw was the problem. Through the protracted battle the line simply slipped into the "gap" cutting the fragile mono.

I watched carefully as "Rib" double looped the 2 lb-test and finished with a reverse clinch knot. From there on out I netted a hat trick of silver torpedos. Another idea is snelling the hook shank. The leader runs directly through the eye, preventing the line from slipping into the gap.

If you haven't learned how to tie a sliding snell, it's time you did. Believe me, it's a valuable tool to have in your arsenal of connections. I use the snell loop to hold skein eggs on the hook shank. Of course it's easier to use a No. 10 treble, but there are times when a single hook will keep your prize from escaping. Also, the loop can be used to attach "attractor" or puff of fluorescent yarn above artificial spawn or spawn bags. Just clip an inch, cinch it to the shank and you're in business.

Another valuable setup for fishing troubled/snag-filled waters in a rig borrowed from the surfing ranks. It employs a slip sinker rig instead of a fixed dropper weight. When a hang up occurs, the running sinker/slip sinker slides up the line, freeing the outfit. The leader is attached to the main monofilament using a Size 8 barrel swivel. Before knotting the heavy line to the second eyelet, thread another swivel on the mono. Add a drop line of 5 inches to the sliding swivel. Now pinch enough split shot to tick bottom regularly. I use this rig with flies and find it works well.

As steelhead home on parent streams, anglers should switch to an outfit similar to the surf rig described above with minor modifications. When rainbows cruise rivermouth regions they're searching out the bars, troughs and ledges which serve as navigational guideposts in their upstream migration. Two to three years earlier, as smolts, these same steelhead were imprinted with river "scent" and through a complex series of olfactory functions the mature fish moves shoreward. By timing your arrival, the surfer has his way with a variety of salmonids, yet taking steelhead requires the bait be in the target zone . . . 3 to 6 inches off bottom, no more.

Sounds pretty exacting. That's what I thought the first time I probed the azure blue troughs of Lake Michigan near Platte Point, Benzie County. It was October 17th and the big lake was in one of its fitful moods. For two days and nights a

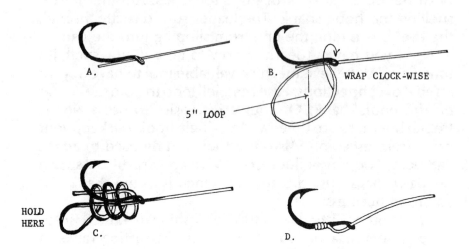

Figure 31. Snelling prevents fraying line during extended battle. (Note: All wraps clock-wise)

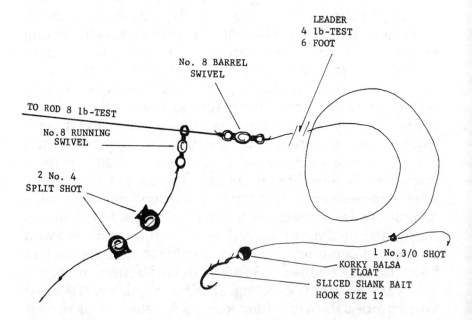

Figure 32. Running swivel keeps lead away from fish throughout contest. Float suspends spawn off bottom where fish can see bait.

25 knot on-shore breeze lashed the coastline. Finally, on the third day the gale broke and all up and down the beach salmon, cohos and kings, porpoised freely.

When I launched a skein of raw spawn at daylight the lake was dead calm. Momentarily, the bait drifted downward. Now came the waiting and waiting. Over the next hour fishermen to my left and right landed a mixture of coho and steelhead, but I drew a blank. My partner Bob Ellis, however, landed two steelhead, no salmon.

At first I thought it was the bit of marshmallow that made the difference, so I hung a sweet morsel and went back to work. Bob was working on his third fish, so I cleared my line and waited.

Once the sleek rainbow was in the mesh I checked his rig. Three or four inches above the hook was a single jawed split shot and below that was a bit of painted cork. The trick was out and Bob filled me in.

"These steelhead cruise with their bellies just off the sandy bottom. They're feeding on eggs dropped by migrating coho. If you get out of that zone, they don't even see your bait! Your skein is way too high." I quickly rigged the 4 pound-test leader and arched the bait lakeward.

Minutes later I was battling my first fish, a silver coho. I lowered the split shot and you guessed it, the second prize was a 4 pound plus steelhead. By 11 o'clock, light levels rose and the action ended. The lesson, oh what a difference an inch or two makes.

When lake waters are calm I prefer the slip-sinker rig, because the swivel rides up the main line mono away from the action. But, on occasion lake seiches make it just about impossible to keep baits on bottom. That's when I thread an egg sinker in the 3/8 to 1/2 ounce class on the main line monofilament. The weight holds the bait in the rolling surf, and when a steelhead strikes, the running mono slips through the center without hesitation. If a rainbow feels any resistance, he'll drop the bait.

Rigging for plug drifting follows the lines of traditional bottom bouncing setups, but with shorter leaders and longer drop lines. Since lures are worked against currents, weights must be capable of holding "divers" stationary. Depending on lure style, drop lines should be 10 to 12 inches long and one half the poundage of main line monos. Typical weights are 3/8 to 1/2 ounce bell sinkers, attached with a barrel snap swivel, size 8.

Leaders should be long enough to permit the lure to "dig" vertically and horizontally. This side to side movement triggers (excites) the steelhead into striking and is extremely important. I will cover this tactic thoroughly in Chapter 9 — Boating River Steelhead — Exciter Fishing, so for now I'll recommend a leader 36 to 42 inches. There are times in late season (early May) when longer leaders are needed, but they are the exception rather than the rule.

CHAPTER 9
BOATING RIVER STEELHEAD
EXCITER FISHING

When Emil Dean, often considered the grandpappy of midwestern riverboat guides, introduced his famous Drop Back method of plugging winter steelhead in 1975, it literally took the angling public by storm. Here was a simplistic method of probing big rivers in late fall or winter which paid big dividends in trophy rainbows, if an angler took the time to read the currents and put his lure in front of resting fish.

Under normal circumstances cold water steelhead are essentially dormant fish. Hugging the bottom they feed little and move even less, but they can be probed into action with deep diving lures such as Tadpollies, Hot N Tots, Hot Shots, Flatfish, etc. Long before Exciter fishing became fashionable Stan Lievense, then a Fisheries Biologist and now retired Resource Specialist from Traverse City, Michigan, began working with a series of lures (spoons and spinners) designed to entice spring steelhead into striking even though they are non-feeding fish.

Stan's theory was based on his pioneering work with temperature fishing (optimum range during which game fish consistently feed-published *Outdoor Life*, April, May, 1971). "We've found steelhead and other salmonids strike regularly when water temperatures are in the 50 degree range. But what about those times when river temperatures are 38 to 40 degrees? The fish must feed, maintain themselves or die. It's that simple."

Equipped with Stan's theory and plenty of cold weather gear, steelheaders in Michigan, Canada and other Great Lakes States began to hook and land large numbers of record rainbows. Ultimately, with Lievense's collaboration, a book entitled "Exciter Fishing" was published and today the tactic has spread to nearly every part of the U.S. and Canada where the mighty *gairdneri* calls home.

As Dean intended, Drop Back or Exciter fishing was developed to attract fish during the period December-March, but it's also very successful in spring (April and May) when the big trout are spawning.

Behaviorally, spring steelhead are non-feeders. Their upstream migrations are directed toward renewing the species and despite occasional lapses in character, rainbows on redds are tough to hook. Drift after drift with spawn or flies may bring an occasional strike, yet the fish is only protecting territory, not feeding.

On numerous occasions I've worked spawning steelhead to the point of exhaustion, walked away, only to have another angler take my place and within minutes hook and land the fish. Some of the luck is blind, but experienced rainbow chasers know patience puts the advantage in your corner time after time.

When probing redd areas, those uniform gravel stretches 1 to 3 feet deep, steer a wide path around the suspected zone, cut the engine and drift into position. Quietly lower the anchor when the craft is approximately 20 yards above the spawning zone. Steelhead are easily

Figure 33.   St. Joe River guide Winn Wolf shows male steelhead taken on Hot-N-Tot, a top Exciter plug.

spooked by excessive noise (including churning props) so stealth is important. Now "drop" or drift the lure downstream, letting the current do the work. Measure the distance by striping line with your left hand. I usually start with 5 (15 ft.) adding 5 more (30 ft.) until the run is covered. Of course, if fish are visible, open the bail, release line until the lure is right on the steelheads nose.

During low water periods (late May and early winter) the lure can be worked on bottom without additional weight. Just attach the diver to your mainline using a quality, snap-swivel and start drifting. But during spring and early fall, when river currents are up, a drop weight must be used to get the lure in the target zone.

Begin the "plunking" setup by knotting your main line mono (8 to 10 pound-test) to one eye of a three-way swivel, size 10. Now knot a 10 to 12 inch section of 4 lb or 6 lb-test mono to the second eyelet. This is the drop line. Depending on current speed, attach either a 3/8 to 1/2 ounce bell sinker to the mono using a reverse clinch knot. If a snag occurs during the "drop" the lighter mono breaks, saving the swivel, plus lure.

The leader is attached last. Forty inches is standard. This length allows the plug to work vertically and horizon-tally — both are important to "exciting" steelhead on redds.

After the lure has worked the run for several minutes, top to bottom, direct the rod tip left or right. The plug will follow and you'll be able to cover a larger area from one locale. If the gravel is extremely wide, start the outboard and push the boat sideways, across the current. By shortening the anchor cable, the craft will slide easily — left or right.

As the lures work, watch your rod tip. It should throb rhythmically. If not, retrieve the plug immediately. Periodically drifting debris may foul the hooks, killing lure action.

The first time I plugged river steelhead on Michigan's Big Manistee River eight years ago I had nothing but trouble. First the hooks fouled. I switched the hanger rig on the U-20 silver flatfish to two trebles, solving the problem. Next came the algae.

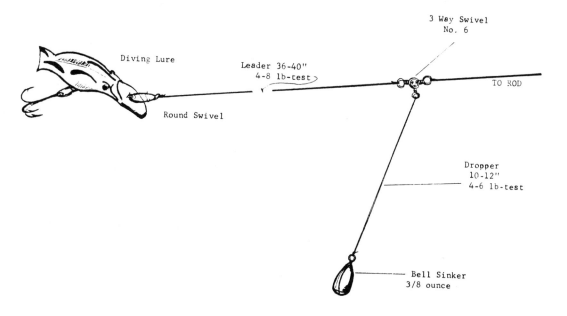

Figure 34.   Standard "plunking" rig for both spring and fall steelhead.
Vary weight to keep lure on bottom.

During the fall thousands of chinook and coho salmon move into the headwaters of the Big M near Tippy Dam. Spawning complete they soon die. Weeks later, their decaying bodies enrich river currents and rock-clinging algae like *Cladaphora*, bloom in profusion. Every time the plug bumped bottom action died.

Lengthening the leader and dropper put the flatfish above the gravel and I immediately hooked an 8 pound female fresh from Lake Michigan. Then, everything went dead. In the subdued early morning light, my 6 pound test leader worked fine, but as light levels rose, the fish became leader shy. Tip. When working turbid waters 6 pound monos are more than adequate. For clear conditions, however, 4 pound should be used.

Under critical conditions 2 pound-test leaders are okay, if you finesse the steelhead early in the battle and use tough, hard-finish monos. Spring fish don't always belt your plug as fall rainbows, so you'll have to set the hooks. Once the trout clamps down, lift the rod tip, pointing the butt at the fish. The rod's shock absorber action plus line stretch should bury the barbs. Tip number 2 — keep those trebles needle-sharp.

After hookup, raise the anchor and drift with the steelhead. By moving at current speed, it's tough for the rainbow to apply leverage against the fragile mono. Using this tactic I've landed many heavyweight rainbows on 2 and 4 pound-test leaders.

Spawning complete, steelhead drop downstream into deep holes, slicks and runs. Here they rest and feed replenishing body fats lost during reproduction. For anglers able to read river currents these fish can be taken, but it's finesse fishing with light leaders (4 and 6 lb-test) and small to medium diving plugs.

In searching out these holding waters, keep one thing in mind. Steelhead are creatures of comfort. Instead of lying in main current tongues they rest along eddies where flows wash food into the lie, and maintaining position requires little effort. Never look for fish holding on or over sandbars, but look for them at current edges or near pocket water. These lies can be created by anything obstructing current flow, i.e. boulders, submerged log, fallen trees, stumps or sweepers attached to the river bank.

Additionally, a slow, deep run along a bank is an ideal spot for resting or feeding rainbows. The tail end of a fast run is also good, as are small deep pockets immediately upstream or downstream from a gravel bar, particularly in late winter when false spawning steelhead ascend rivers.

Probing these selective niches, pockets require a slow deliberate presentation and nowhere is the technique more developed than on west coast rivers such as the Umpqua, Deschutes, Smith, Hood or Coquille Rivers. Here, the method is sometimes nick-named "bug" drifting or in industry parlance, Hot Shotting.

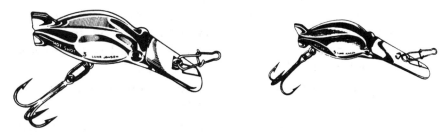

Figure 35. Successful technique for early and late steelhead is "Hot Shotting". Number 30 dives to 12 ft. (left). Smaller No. 50 to 10 ft. (Dwg. courtesy Luhr Jensen).

Developed by the Luhr Jensen group, this style of Exciter fishing uses a self-planing diving lure to reach bottom hugging steelhead. For years the technique was used exclusively by professional drift boat guides, so a lot of the "secrets" of How-To were closely guarded secrets, but that's changed in recent years.

Basically, the plugs are rigged with round-ended snaps (no swivels-permitting complete freedom) and no weight. By proper adjustment the "bug" will track downward. Once on bottom its path and downstream movement is controlled by the drift boat operator. Actually, Hot Shotting (including Drop Back) can be practiced from any type of craft, but for slow, exacting work the Drift or Double-ended McKenzie boat is preferred.

As with "Drop Back," start well above holding water with the boat headed upstream. Row or motor just fast enough to hold against the current. The key to success is a slow and deliberate presentation. As the lure moves downstream (40 to 60 feet from craft) it follows current paths to holding steelhead. If no strike occurs, skirt the drift (particularly on productive waters) wait a few minutes and repeat the process. The second time around just might trigger a response.

The throbbing rod tip shows the lure is working properly and on bottom. The boat's downstream drift should be slow enough to maintain plug action. If not, hold the craft steady and let the current go to work. Occasionally drifters anchor above productive runs and allow the "bug" to probe every pocket. If there's a steelhead resting there, sooner or later he'll be irritated into striking.

When rigging hot shots keep in mind the lighter the line, the less water friction and the quicker the plug will reach bottom. The standard for UL steelheading is 8 pound-test with 4 and 6 lb. leaders of Maxima, Trilene XT or Stren monofilament. A single barrel swivel is tied into the leader 36 inches from the lure. This keeps the line from twisting and fouling the plug. Plus, lure action is enhanced.

The most popular size Hot Shots are the #20 (3 1/4") and smaller #30 (2 5/8"). For winter steelhead the larger 20 is preferred. The 20 dives to 18 feet, while the 30 dives to 12 feet. Both sizes are fine, if they track correctly.

Factory direct the lure should dive straight and true, but occasionally some adjustment may be necessary. Drop the plug into river currents and watch its lateral movement. If the "bug" runs to one side you'll need to do some tinkering. For left divers, simply turn the screw eye slightly clockwise using needle nose pliers or similar. Check the results,

Figure 36. For slow, exacting drop-back trolling it's hard to beat double end McKenzie boat. Watch rod tips for correct lure action. (Dwg. courtesy Luhr Jensen).

then run the lure back. For right divers adjust the front eye slightly counterclockwise. This fine "tuning" will make all the difference in fish attracted and hooked.

As with the drop back tactic, steelhead striking a Hot Shot usually hook themselves, if trebles are sharp. You can sharpen the standard hooks or replace them with a lighter one. Fine wire trebles increase lure action, but may need changing after landing a heavy fish. If you decide to use the lighter version, I recommend Eagle Claw's #375, Size #4 treble.

Of the many plug finishes (Drop Back or Hot Shotting) available for steelheading the most popular are metallic dark green, metallic blue, gold, silver prism/ blue scale and silver prism/green scale. In low, gin-clear waters darker finishes are more productive including black, silver/black scale, green prism/black scale, blue prism/black scale. When river currents are turbulent try hot colors such as a chartreuse/ red dot or fluorescent red/black spots. Recently a number of manufacturers have added "glo in the dark" phosphorous finishes (phosphorus/green top and phos./blue top) and have proven successful in low light, high water conditions.

Even though the tactics described here were designed for boaters, both drop back and hot shotting can be successfully practiced by wade fishermen. Rigging is identical to "plunking," but dropper weight is increased to hold the plug stationary.

Wade into position above the lie and cast the lure quartering downstream. As the plug reaches the target zone, close the bail. The sinker should hold the diver in one spot, if not add more lead. Keep the rod tip at a 20 d. angle and watch the action. After several minutes, raise the rod and let the plug work downstream a foot or so. Repeat the process until the run is covered or until a steelhead smashes the "bug." Keep a good grip on that prized spin outfit when drifting and dropping. More than one steelheader has been shocked numb when his graphite stick disappeared beneath the boiling currents — don't let it happen to you.

CHAPTER 10
WATER TYPES AND
HOW TO FISH THEM

People who fish steelhead year round (spring, summer and fall) have definite preferences (methods and areas) and most, if not all, are based on past personal experience or recommendations of angling buddies. It's been that way since I began dredging light leaders for *anadromous* rainbows, and the practice will continue into the foreseeable future. Chances are excellent that if you take a steelhead from a particular lie one season the following year the episode can be repeated, if you show up at the same calendar time and do basically the same thing. Success begets success and the story goes on. But, what about those exploring souls who strike out in new paths and directions looking for steelhead? These pioneers have a consistent ace-in-the-hole working for them and it's called Stream Savvy.

Back in Chapter 4, Tackle and Tactics, I briefly covered the aspects of drifting and reading steelhead waters. Here, I want to continue and build on the theme of Predic-

119

tion and Interpretation, for it's through these basic premises the trouter leaves the ranks of the trial and error artist and moves into the ranks of the expert. I did it. So can you.

Recapping, steelhead follow the same basic migration routes from year to year and unless there is a drastic shift in river bottoms, these same paths and lies continue to attract silver immigrants each year, including salmon.

As the giant rainbows enter rivermouth regions they are basically feeding fish and as such take up stream lies affording both comfort and food. In other words, they select those deep runs and glides which enable them to feed with the least effort. Now, with sufficient waters covering their upstream movement, overhead protection is not a primary concern. But, as they enter spawning waters upstream this pattern shifts.

Instead of feeding, the species concentrates on reproduction. Additionally, the need for cover becomes paramount. Spawning steelhead sense their vulnerability in headwater gravels and select those stream lies offering suitable nest building close to protective covers. During clear water periods the average steelheader has no problem locating and hooking steelhead, but what about those periods when rivers run higher than normal, thus erasing the clues as to where the fish are. Now is when a degree in Stream Reading is worth its weight in gold.

Basically, the program goes something like this. Surface waters reflect the underlying benthos (bottom) structure. If topside currents flow smooth, uninterrupted and fast, chances are excellent the bottom is clean, with no obstructions, and the surface speed is about the same as those on bottom. Put a log, stump or rock in the waterway, and an equal volume of water will be displaced, thus forming pocket water for migrating/feeding steelhead, either in front of, under or behind the object.

If surface currents run choppy, the visual image below is one of many obstructions and bottom currents are slowed considerably. Deep runs and depressions usually show smooth surfaces and darker water, yet these areas can

Figure 37. Smooth water behind angler indicates possible spawning water and signals FISH HERE.

be deceiving. The only sure way of knowing exactly what's on bottom is through visual inspection (during low water or snorkeling in summer) or by keeping a river map showing changes in bottom strata. Over the years, I've logged a diary with up to date conditions on several waterways and it's paid off many times.

In order to aid the beginning UL fan I've illustrated three basic river types and how fish utilize them. Then, I take you on an overhead tour of my favorite steelheading waters. By diagraming how to read and probe each, hopefully you'll have a better handle on approaching your own rainbow river. Remember, however, timing your arrival to coincide with peak migrations is as important to success as reading water wisely.

If there's an example of typical steelheading waters in the midwest, the Muskegon River, central Newaygo County, has to be it. Long, wide with alternating stretches of gravelly runs and pools the stream hosts an excellent run of silver bullets every spring and fall. Over the seasons I've grown particularly fond of the upper reaches of the "river of marshes" and know the stream well enough to consistently find fish, and if the luck is with me land a few.

Beginning in early March steelhead push into river-mouth regions of Muskegon Lake on Lake Michigan and within days begin the migration to headwater gravel some 35 plus miles inland. Throughout their journey the fish utilize deep runs and pools for resting and feeding. Then, as water temperatures warm into the low and mid 40's, the "hord" start territorializing spawning gravel. For the fishermen knowing these holding waters, pre-season angling here can be outstanding.

Approximately 4 miles below the dam at Croton, the early season angler can find fish in any one of a series of deep runs, holes and glides. In Illustration 1, I show a typical 1 1/2 mile stretch of the river and where fish normally hold. In the uppermost pool (Powers) Section A, steelhead consistently rest in the deepest portion of the water, moving little to intercept drifting baits. Here, the angler must present his

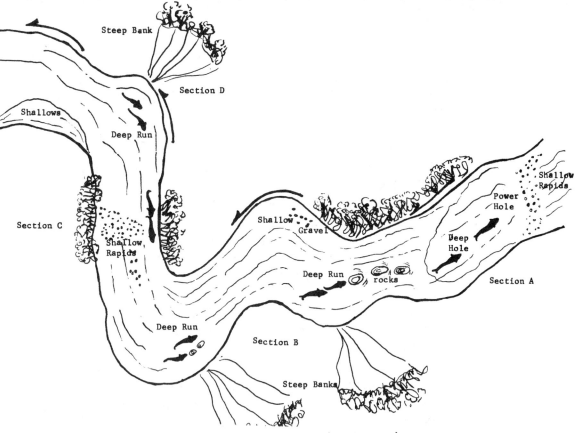

Figure 38. 1½ mile section of Muskegon River showing early season lies.

bait in the least threatening way and literally hit the rainbow right on the chops, otherwise, the wait between hookups, even with light leaders can be a long one. Exploration is the only way to find these fish.

Moving further downstream the deep runs along the twin steep banks (Section B) also harbor resting, migrating steelhead. One day these waters can be hot, the next cold. Fish normally hold up in front of or behind the large rocks on the outside or "shallow" portion of the run. Working these waters is tough for the drift fisherman, simply because the searching leader finds rocks before fish, foiling a drag free presentation. But, for the boater using exciter tactics (Chapter 9) it's an easy task to work a wobbling diver right into a fish's waiting jaws.

Occasionally the shallow rapids (Section C) produces an early fish, but the deep run (Section D) below is more productive. Why? Because it's holding water for fish waiting to spawn in the gravel stretch immediately upstream. Again, the bait must hit the fish right on the nose or you're out of business.

As river temperatures warm to the mid to high 40's steelhead begin occupying the spawning gravel located in Section C of the river. I've enlarged this stretch of water (Illustration 2) to show exactly where fish rest and spawn. Also, I list the best drift lanes and rod positions for the angler.

Basic Water Coverage

In Position No. 1, steelhead often lie in front of, behind or beside mid-stream rocks. Most of these stones are submerged, but during low water the tops are visible. Surface waters here are choppy, with an occasional downstream boil. The angler should work this area with a short leader (4 ft.), placing his casts adjacent to the rocks. The bait should be "on bottom" throughout the drift.

Position 2 has an occasional large rock deflecting the deep flowing currents, so the surface here is much smoother, with an intermittent top boil showing. Steelhead rest in this region and by running a longer, searching leader (5 ft.) the angler can hook fish from the shallow side, keeping the action directly in front of him.

Figure 39.   Blown up, overhead view of Section C showing where fish rest and spawn.

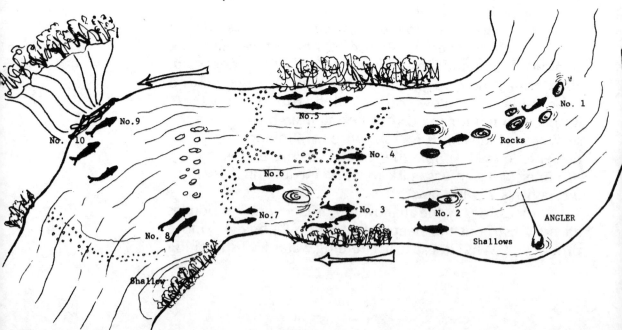

Once steelhead move into positions 3, 4, 5 & 7, it's possible to fish to visible targets, but if the water's turbid (discolored) it's a realtively simple matter to keep your bait in the proper zone. The clue is the smooth surface water. A uniformly graveled bottom (spawning territory) runs clean, fast and uninterrupted. The depth in Position 3 varies from 3 ft. to 18 inches, so getting on bottom is easy using one No. 4 split-shot. By running a long leader (6 ft. +) it's possible to consistently hook fish if the drift is conducted methodically.

Begin by quartering your casts upstream directly in front of your position and follow the drift downstream. Then renew the cast. Probe the each line 4 to 5 times, then lengthen the monofilament a yard or so and return. Watch for the "strike" in the smooth water below. It will be little more than a brief hesitation, a lull in the drift, so keep slack to a minimum. When it occurs, just lift the rod tip up and back. This should be sufficient to set the hook. Let the fish have its head initially, then, apply steady pressure, pointing the rod butt at the fish at all times. Ten to twelve minutes should be adequate time to land your prize.

At Position No. 4, steelhead rest in deep pockets located at mid-river. The surface here is smooth and like Position 3, keep your offering on bottom. No strike? Take a few steps downstream and renew the drift. Eventually you'll hit the target zone and fish on is assured. Remember, watch for the hesitation.

No. 5 presents another situation. The smooth gravel bottom here is reflected in surface waters, so steelhead use this area for nest building. Yet, bank/wading fishermen have a tough time with the brush-infested shoreline. Here, the angler should work from an anchored boat. Place your craft directly across from the lie, and run your offering through. Keep the leader short (4 ft.) and you'll have better casting accuracy, plus control over each drift.

Below the smooth water stretches, Position No. 6, rainbows rest in the deep hole just off shore. A boiling surface indicates submerged rocks and boulders below. Since the area provides protection, spawning fish retreat here when danger threatens. Drifting No. 6 is best done below Position No. 3. Hold the rod tip high and spill line from the spool. Work your offering repeated through and around this area. At mid-day these lies can be very productive.

Position 7 is another smooth surface run indicating spawning gravel. Steelhead use this area in early morning and late evening. Lob your bait below the rock and follow the drift. Repeat the process until you've covered the water thoroughly. In shallow currents, spawning rainbows are easily seen against the polished bottom. I use amber-tinted polaroids to increase visibility in low light. You can do the same.

When fish at No. 7 are disturbed they usually drop into protective waters at Position No. 8. Here, surfaces are choppy (reflecting a rock covered bottom) so steelhead feel safe. By standing at No. 7 and spilling line, No. 8 can be thoroughly covered. I've taken fish by letting the bait hang in the current, but drifting is better. Use a searching leader in the 5 foot range to locate resting fish.

Across river, below the steep bank, steelhead rest in deep water (Position No. 9) during daytime and move into spawning gravel (No. 5) in mornings and evenings. This zone is reached by wading beyond Position No. 8 and quartering your rig upstream to No. 9 and following the drift downstream. At surface the river runs slightly choppy, mirroring a rocky bottom, with intermittent clear stretches. Currents are slower in the tail end of the glide and this presents a problem. Initially the drift flows smoothly, then hangs up. The solution? A bobber rig set at 5 foot with a 3 foot leader.

The shoreline below the steep banks is cluttered with drift debris and extends into the currents (No. 10). Steelhead retreat to this cover during the day and the only way to dig them out is drifting a bobber by the barrier. The searching leader puts your offering under the logs where a rainbow can jump on it. Standard 3-way swivel setups will also work, but be prepared to lose a few rigs.

Forty miles north of the mighty Muskegon there's

another steelheading favorite of mine, the Big Manistee River. The Big M supports an excellent run of giant rainbows both spring and fall, but fishing the river is tough. It is (as the name suggests) large water. Its levels fluctuate morning and night (site of Tippy Hydroelectric Dam), plus the bottoms are a nightmarish jumble of sunken logs and stumps. Excellent hiding and feeding lies for foraging steelhead, but a head-ache to successfully probe.

The first time I fished Tippy Dam I came away mumbling to myself. Within an hour after I began drifting my chartreuse bodied mayfly nymph, water levels rose and the fishing went to zero. I retreated to the Wellston Inn on M 52 at Wellston, Michigan, to get the lowdown. The resident expert Frank Lendzion told me I'd have to hit the river during low water from daylight to 10:00 o'clock and from 1:30 p.m. to 5:30. That's when the generators are down and fishing is up. I took his advise and ever since I've reaped the harvest of silver torpedos at Tippy.

Dam sites produce excellent angling for a number of reasons. First, steelhead search out well-oxygenated stream lies, and the churning waters at the base of a hydroelectric operation of any dam mix tremendous amounts of oxygen with water. Secondly, the water temperature there is usually constant, remaining 38 to 45 degrees (depending on the season) which attracts fish. Thirdly, salmonids, in their upstream surge are stopped by the dam. Steelhead, therefore, congregate near the structure or in deep holes downstream.

First-timers at a dam site are usually confused as to where the fish are, so I've prepared a bird's eye view of the Tippy site (Illustration 3) showing how steelhead position themselves below a hydro dam, and suggest how each position is best fished.

Below the brow or breast of Tippy the flume ports push water against the piers, resulting in a clock-wise or counter-clockwise movement of river currents. This cushion of "warm" water is attractive to migrating steelhead (parti-cularly in early spring and early winter) and the fish position

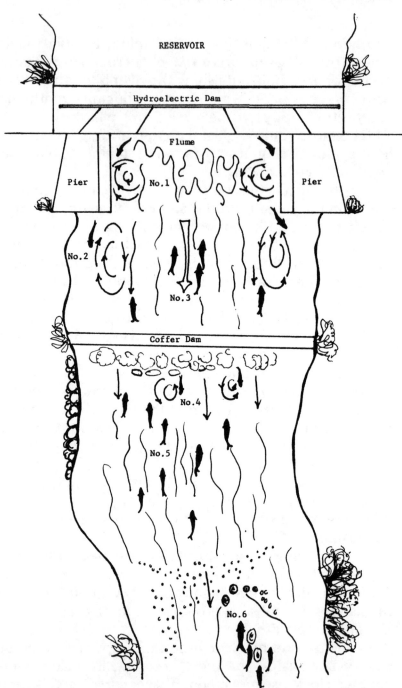

Figure 40. Overhead view of hydroelectric dam and how steelhead use site. (Tippy Dam, Manistee River).

themselves, head in the current, feeding on drifting tidbits.

Position No. 1 is boat fishing only. Typically, anglers anchor adjacent to the circular currents and cast their weighted rigs into boil and let it work. Or they float a bobber. I've found this location to be productive, but not nearly as good as Nos. 2 and 3.

As center currents (No. 3) rush downstream another eddy is set up immediately below the piers. This sidewash is much gentler than its upstream counterpart and requires a bobber to "float" your bait to waiting steelhead. Again, fish position themselves, head into the current, so your bait must go with the flow. Establish the depth, set your bobber so the wiggler or spawn bag rides just off-bottom. Launch the rig up or downstream (as the backwash flows) and follow the bobber with the rod tip. Spill line to extend the drift if necessary. When the bobber dips or pops sideways strike quickly.

Position No. 3 is more suited to traditional bottom bouncing rigs incorporating a 3-way swivel and enough split-shot to tick bottom. Your leader here should be long (5 to 6 ft.), but on the heavy side, 6 pound-test. When a steelhead is hooked in fast currents, it's tough to turn their head against the current, and when you do the wide tail and body puts excessive strain on thin monos. Probe the outside edges of the center arrow for best results.

Below the Coffer Dam, tumbling currents create pocket eddies and like the steelhead adjacent to upstream Piers they face the current. Position 4 is another prime location for bobber fishing, because the float permits "stalling" the downstream drift long enough to attract a feeding fish. Cast your offering into the eddy. Lift rod tip high overhead and wait for the strike. By clearing the mono from surface currents the bait can work freely. After several minutes drop the rod tip downward. Currents will drag the bobber downstream over new water. As the offering moves, keep the line slack-free. Then you'll have a direct hooking route.

In spring literally hundreds of silver steelhead load up below the coffer and Position 5 is an excellent place to ply a standard 4 pound-test rig. Here, I usually run a 4 1/2 to five foot leader with good results. Since there will be other anglers on either side of you, cover the water by extending casts in and out.

Continuing downstream to Position 6 the angler finds another hotspot, but tough to fish. A deep, long glide over irregular bottoms calls for a bobber setup. Without it, you'll spend most of the time re-rigging. On my last trip to the Bobber Hole (April 24th) I hooked 5 fish, landing 3. Nickle-size spawn clusters, drifting five feet down did the trick.

Small Stream Basics

In spite of the fact that many of our steelhead rivers across the U.S. are big, brawling waterways requiring current reading to be successful, just as many or perhaps more are small streams, averaging a scant 35 to 45 feet wide. These "creeks" abound in headwater country in the midwest and in my area of southwest Michigan, they contribute significantly to the steelhead fishery.

Finding fish in these streams is usually a matter of showing up at peak migration periods and dredging a line. The water is shallow, clear and despite the fact that most are brushy and closed in, it's surprising how successful the UL steelheader can be here, if he presents his offering correctly and at the right time of day.

The first time I witnessed small creek strategy was some eight years ago. The location was a crystalline stretch of the Platte River near Honor, Michigan. The angler was Tom Naumes, a trouter from Bellaire and although Tom was using a 9 1/2 foot flyrod, his leader tippet was tapered to 5X (4 lb-test). During an hour session on a 200 yard section of the Platte, Naumes hooked 5 fish, landing 3. One was a female in 10 pound class, the others 5 to 6 pounders.

The ticket that April 4th morning was a Skykomish fly pattern dredged next to barriers (i.e., log jams, rocks, mid-stream pockets and deep holes) which might hide steelhead. In Illustration 4 I show a scaled down version of the river and where steelhead position themselves.

The key to successful small steelheading is arriving

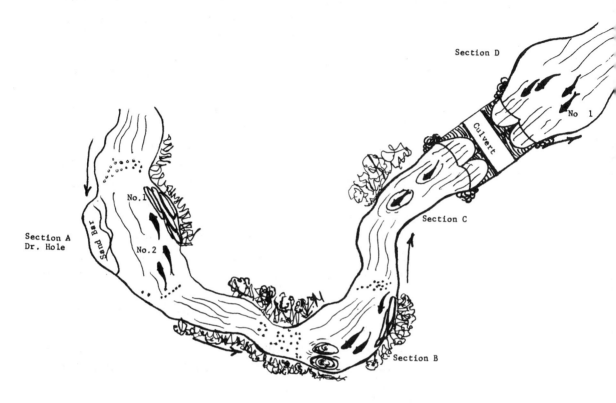

Figure 41. Overhead view of small stream lies and how steelhead position themselves. (Scaled section of Plate River, Honor, Mich.)

early (daybreak) and working your offering "on bottom." In Section A, Dr. Hole, Tom repeatedly worked his fly adjacent to the log jam opposite the sand bar. By casting upstream and quickly mending the drift, fish were hooked at Position 1 and in the tail of the lie, Position 2. As light levels rose the action tapered sharply. In the Drs., 3 fish were hooked, 1 landed.

When we arrived at Section B, it was 9:30 a.m. and the fish had retreated to a lie below several large rocks. Most were anchored next to or under a log stream deflector. When I quizzed Tom on how he planned on snaking them out. His only reply was, "Watch!" Moments later the amber bodied spring nymph fly was dangling in front of a resting fish. Wham! Fish on.

In both Sections A and B, my partner ran a short leader in the 36 to 40 inch range. At B, Naumes lowered his No. 7 split-shot within a foot of the fly and "dabbed" the offering on the steelhead's nose, much like a carriage driver would entice a horse with carrots. I couldn't believe it, but here was "exciter" fishing with flies.

Section C was revealed through our polaroids. In the bright sunlight mid-stream pockets showed dark against the light gravel bottom. By lob casting, each position was systematically probed, and on the tenth cast a sleek female in the 5 pound class nailed Tom's shaggy nymph and it was off to the races.

As with the other steelhead, Naumes let the rainbow have its head and once it was beyond the "panic" stage, he coaxed and led the fish through several acrobatic runs finally beaching it against his boots. I was impressed.

By 11:30 a.m. we'd reached the 4 wheel-drive, and thinking the fishing was over I dismantled my flyrod. "Not yet," Naumes encouraged. "This culvert hole (Section D) has produced a number of big steelhead lately. Why don't you give it a try?"

Tom coached, while I worked the hot orange Skykomish Sunrise fly. Basically, it was vertical fishing with a flyrod. Twenty drifts or so and I nailed an 8 pound male steelhead at Position 1. When it jumped we were eyeball to eyeball five feet up! I don't know who was more surprised! Another 10 minutes and I netted my prize.

CHAPTER 11
SURF FISHING STEELHEAD

Less than a decade ago the surf fisherman's private world was the exclusive domain of saltwater anglers, but no more. Along Great Lakes shores, rivermouths and beaches fishermen have finally succumbed to the spell of the surf. Probing the charging waves trouters search out *Salmo gairdneri,* the mighty steelhead.

On a day to day basis the big fish are not easy to locate. Except at the peak of their runs, steelhead are scattered. Wind, weather and water conditions, i.e., temperature and clarity, affect the fish greatly, making them more or less susceptible to angling techniques — therein lies the challenge. To be successful the surfer must be both hunter and fisherman. He must have the savvy to find the bars, troughs and points, then be able to present his offering in such a way that migrating fish cannot resist it.

Sounds easy enough, and in most cases is, but like many outdoor endeavors being in the right place at the right time can make a difference. My first experience with steelhead in the surf was a prime example of opportunism at its best. My wife Joan and I were working a turquoise trough near the mouth of the Platte River west of Honor, Michigan. The day was a gem. A bright sun hung high overhead, but the air temperatured registered a cool 52 degrees F. It was 10:00 a.m., May 4th. Since 5 that morning we'd pounded the river trying to find a late-run steelhead. The few fish we did locate spurned every offering, so we decided to check the surf.

A stiff on-shore breeze was at work as I launched a skein of raw spawn into the target zone. The bait slipped beneath the undulating seiches and the waiting began. Minutes later a heavy-bodied steelhead rocketed from the lake's emerald surface. Until I felt the surge on my line the rainbow appeared free, then with terrifying speed the fish dispelled that thought. The monofilament quickly melted from the closed-face spincast reel as the steelhead made a wide, sweeping turn and raced shoreward. The fish shook its head furiously above the boiling waves and dropped back into the trough. A quick run to the right, again a cascading leap. Ten more minutes and the steelhead came gasping on its side. In one sweeping motion Joan slipped the broad-hooped net under the silver fish and lifted it high above the clear water.

Before 2 o'clock that afternoon Joan and I hooked a total of 7 fish, landing 3. The biggest pulled the scale down an even 11 pounds. Even though brilliant skies, clear water and warm temperatures were against us that day, we still caught fish. There were, however, other factors working in our favor.

First, the steelhead at Platte Point were seeking ideal water temperatures. As winds pushed river currents shoreward, mingling lake and stream waters created a suitable niche for cruising fish. Second, warmer river temperatures attracted baitfish such as smelt and alewife (trout and salmon feed heavily on this forage base in Spring), thus steelhead were concentrated, searching for food. Finally, the trough in question was deep enough to provide cover for migrating

Figure 42.   River mouth regions are productive surf locations for heavy-weight steelhead, spring and fall.

steelhead. Put it all together and we had an ideal, red-letter day that any steelheader would long remember.

Fifteen years ago, when midwestern trout and salmon programs were getting on track, few anglers considered surfing let alone try it. The idea of standing waist-deep in one of the Great Lakes seemed ludicrous, yet today literally thousands of steelheaders march to a different drummer when rainbows enter the surf.

Compared to their river counterparts steelhead in rivermouths are easy to catch. Cruising shorelines, the fish feed constantly. Stomach autopsies show steelhead gorge themselves on available food stocks (baitfish or single eggs dropped by migrating salmon/trout). One would think such random and often savage feeding behavior has a measured effect on their acceptance of a properly presented bait, yet that's not the case.

As one sage of the surfing clan observed recently, "catching a steelhead is easy once you locate him. All you have to do is launch a bait, then hurry up and wait." And, from personal experience, that's a pretty fair assessment.

One of the most reliable methods I use to find productive surfing sites employs a reconnaissance long before the season begins. By contacting State Fishery Officials, anglers can request planting records of major steelhead and salmon rivers. Heavy fish concentrations/plants in a system should provide a greater ratio of returnees 2 to 3 years later (spring or fall), thus better opportunities.

Other information sources include local steelhead chapters and tackle shops. Quite often productive surfing sites turn on and of quickly. As long as water temperatures (lake and rivermouth) hold in the low 50's and food fish are available, steelhead continue to hug shorelines for extended periods. The duration varies from year to year, but the average period lasts 3 weeks in spring and 2 weeks in fall, sometimes longer.

Initially the spring migration gets under way as warmer river temperatures attract steelhead, usually late March or early April. Cold lake waters direct the giant

rainbows inland and by intercepting this seasonal movement the surfer has his way with the silver horde. Spawning
complete, the fish head downstream once again, (late April
or early May) seeking comfortable lake temperatures.

In fall the reverse process occurs. As river waters cool,
they attract all salmonids (particularly steelhead), and the
trout once again swarm in rivermouth regions. This "false"
spawning run puts thousands of sleek torpedos in front of
anglers for a second time. Getting in on this unexpected
bonanza is simple for anglers having contacts along
shoreline hotspots. All it takes is one phone call.

The first time I surfed the fall steelhead run at
Thompson Creek, at the tip of Lake Michigan, I could do no
wrong. It was late September when Gary Marshall, a Resource Specialist, Michigan Travel Bureau called and said the
surf was red hot near the village of Thompson in Michigan's
upper peninsula. Traditionally, river steelheading in the
upper peninsula doesn't get underway until late October,
but Thompson Creek is unique.

The DNR (Dept. Natural Resources) operates an egg-
taking/hatchery station for coho salmon here, but the fish
aren't the run-of-the-mill Pacific variety, but an early run
Alaskan strain, so they spawn earlier than their west coast
cousins. The steelhead, being opportunists, follow the coho
homing on Thompson Creek, feeding heavily on eggs
dropped by gravid females. So the stage is set for some
fantastic surfing.

The following morning Marshall and I struggled into
cold-weather gear and waders. In the pre-dawn light we
waded waist deep in the metallic-gray surges of Lake
Michigan. I launched a skein of chunk spawn and held my
long rod horizontal to the surface.

A few minutes later my line began to throb. Forty feet
out the surface exploded. Instinctively the rod arched
backward. My drag was set light and the fish took line freely.
Sixty yard slipped through the guides before I could turn the
rainbow, by then the steelhead was dangerously close to
several anchored boats.

Figure 43.   Steelheader Gary Marshall shows mixed catch of coho and
steelhead taken at Thompson Creek, near Manistique, Michigan.
Surfing action is best before and after daybreak.

I pushed the rod butt forward and pressured the 4 pound-test leader to the limit. The silver fish surged right, then raced shoreward. Two electrifying leaps and the fish came in. Grudgingly it gave ground, as I urged the rod back. Finally, the rainbow lay finning on its side. After several attempts I grasped the broad head and lifted 8½ pounds of steelhead from the green lake waters.

Rigging for fall or spring surfing employs a slip sinker setup as described in Chapter 8 — Rigging Methods. To complete the outfit you'll need 2, No. 8 Japanned barrel swivels, 2 or 4 pound test leader spools, wide-bend bait hooks, Size 12 or Size 10 trebles and a selection of shot Size 4, 3/0 and BB, preferably jawed style. This design allows adding and subtracting weight quickly with no damage to fragile monofilaments.

Thread the 8 pound-test running line through the eye of a No. 7 barrel swivel and knot it to the second swivel. Add a drop line (4 pound-test) 5 inches long to the running swivel. Now pinch 2- No. 4 shot to the short length of mono. The lead serves as weight for casting and holding the spawn against wave action. If the surf is up, more shot can be attached.

The leader comes next. Since most surfing locals are relatively snag free, both 2 and 4 pound-test leaders can be used, but I prefer 4. You'll be fishing in a crowd at most sites and using the heavy stuff gets the job done faster. If waters are clouded from surf action, run 6 pound-test.

Spool 4½ to 5 feet of hard-finish monofilament such as Maxima, Stren or Berkley XT Trilene, and knot it to the main line swivel. Double loop all connections for strength and finish with a reverse clinch knot. Remember to moisten each knot with saliva before pulling tight. This improves holding strength 100%.

The recommended method for hook attachment is snelling — for two reasons. First, the knot is stronger. Since the leader runs directly through eye, there's little possibility of the gap cutting the fragile mono. Second, the snell loop allows you to pull the skein tight against the shank. For additional security use a sliced shank hook (bait keeper) single or double.

For convenience I like to pre-cut skein eggs into small chunks (nickel size or larger) so when the action gets underway I'm bending my rod, not scissoring roe. Place the spawn in bait container, hang it around your neck and you're in business. One final tip, working skein eggs is usually a gooey proposition. Keep a small towel handy, you'll need it.

If snelling isn't in your bag of tricks, a treble hook can be used just as effectively. I suggest size 10, or 8. Size 6 is a bit large, but for heavyweight steelhead they provide extra holding power. Drape or wrap the spawn on the shank and it's ready to fish.

Since steelhead are primarily sight feeders spawn bags or skein must be off-bottom, otherwise it'll be a long time between strikes. Remember, in fall rainbows cruise below schooled salmon foraging on eggs. Put the bait too high and you'll take salmon. Too low and it's zip, zero.

There are three methods of floating/buoying surf baits. One uses styrofoam. Another cork. A third marshmallows, the miniature sugar puffs used on deserts and hot chocolate! On the Thompson Creek outing I used marshmallows, yet they had drawbacks. Once water logged, wave action shed the sugar, and it was back to base one.

Today I use a commercial application called "Lil Corky" manufactured by Yakima Bait Company. These epoxy enameled cork floats come in variety of sizes, colors and they're easy to rig. Just thread on the leader, knot the hook and that's it. Size 10s float a skein perfectly and in chartreuse, peach or fluorescent orange they're hard to beat.

If you can't find the corky floats, try a piece of styro-foam (disc or peanut) that's used to pack fragile materials. Snip off a pea-size chunk, impale it on the barb and go for it. Or if you prefer, incorporate the material in a spawn bag. Keep the bait nickel size and you'll take more fish.

Before launching the outfit, pinch a single, jawed split

Figure 44.   Small heads and heafty bodies characterize lake-run steelhead. This fish took skein spawn floated with korky rig.

shot size 3/0 approximately 4 inches from the hook. The weight keeps the bait from floating out of the target zone and in front of cruising steelhead.

During spring surfing session I usually put the 3/0 shot 10 to 12 inches above the hook. Early run fish are schooled and on the move. They orient to bottom structure, but not in the same manner as fall steelhead. Now, the prime consideration is placing the bait off-bottom. Sooner or later the skein "milks" into river/lake waters attracting rainbows. Then, it's usually a matter of which fish will reach the bait first.

Where to launch your offering? Here are a few tips. In spring walk the beach or shoreline near rivermouths noting sand bars, troughs, points and other "structure" which signal a change in lake bottoms. Steelhead cruise these areas in search of comfortable water temperatures and food. Most surfing hotspots will be lined with fishermen showing the way, yet there are times when you may be the first on the scene. If water conditions are clear a pair of polaroids will help locate the target area — otherwise probe the region where river and lake waters mix. Several of my surfing buddies divide their time between spoon chugging and floating eggs, just to pass the time. When a school arrives they switch to the most productive tactic.

Fall surfing is a little more exacting. Since river waters are colder and therefore denser than surrounding lake waters, currents show as "slicks" (smooth areas) against a dark background. In early morning look for these zones and launch your bait.

Since river waters are typically darker than lake or ocean waters it's easy to trace their paths. For instance, the tannic waters of Thompson Creek are easy to spot against the emerald green of Lake Michigan and finding a spot here amounts to following the colored water.

The well established rule of fishing 2 hours after daybreak and 2 hours before dark also applies to surfing steelhead. These fish are keyed to water temperature and what fisheries biologists call negative *phototropism*. In short, migrating rainbows are sensitive to direct light and avoid it.

When the sun is high overhead and water clear most trout seek a comfort zone near deep water. Here, they find both protection and lower light levels. In most instances these areas are out of reach for wade fishermen, but a small cartop boat can put you on them. Overcast periods, combined with strong on-shore breezes should produce action throughout the day.

Since both spring and fall offer steelheaders surfing opportunities it's a toss up as to which period is best. During March and April angling is usually a bone-chilling, single species affair with an occasional salmon thrown in. In fall it can be butter warm or as frigid as a well diggers fanny. I've surfed numerous Great Lake ports in late October when thermometers hovered in the mid to upper 70's, shirt sleeve weather. Then, again I've plucked icicles from guides in September. If you plan on taking steelhead, spring or fall, dress accordingly. A quality insulated wader combined with several layers of down, plus wool gloves and hat give the fisherman a leg up. A long time ago I learned fighting fish and fighting cold doesn't mix.

Given a choice, fall is my favorite surfing time. Warm, colorful days, accompanied by cool nights put a veritable cornucopia of trout in surfing locals. Browns, lakers, coho and king salmon converge on parental/estuary waters and the migration is underway. It's a cycle without end and along with the silver immigrants comes the mighty steelhead. From that point on it's man against fish.

CHAPTER 12
STEELHEADING ACROSS
THE UNITED STATES
AN OVERVIEW

In his lead column as fishing editor for Outdoor Life, October 1968, Joe Brooks wrote a piece entitled "Heaven Is A Steelhead," and with that title captured the essence of the sport. Of course he was speaking of the super star of western streams the Babine River in northern British Columbia, yet no matter where a steelhead is discussed east, midwest or coastal rivers in the Pacific west, he is indeed king of the trout family.

As mentioned in Chapter 2 — Target Fish, the biggest problem of hooking and landing a migrating rainbow is being on a given river at the right time and plying your offering on bottom. If the presentation is correct and the fish in the mood, you're halfway home. In the past so much of trouting, steelheading in particular, was steeped/hidden in deep recesses of tradition, and the taking a silver torpedo was thought of as a herculean feat reserved only for the chosen few. Today, however it's a different story. Any angler wishing to pursue *Salmo gairdneri* can do so on a limited budget, and by doing his homework ahead of time most stand a better than average chance for success.

In order to narrow the field of "possibles" for aspiring rainbow chasers I've put together a list of streams, east, midwest and far west with comments on each, i.e. location, productivity, timing, etc. Specific dates are tough to recommend, but generally speaking, late March to mid April are prime weeks for spring fish, winter fish, December through February.

Midwest

It's a well established fact that rivers in the Great Lakes region maintain, support and give up more mature steelhead than any fishery in the world, including the vast rainbow country of the 49th State, Alaska. Of course the basis of this productivity (to 80% in some rivers) is intensive management, planting hundreds of thousands of fingerlings, both spring and fall. To the tried, die-hard steelheader these fish are inferior to wild specimens and argue against their continued use. On the other hand the average angler welcomes these fish saying "it's better to have fought and lost than not to have fought at all." In the foreseeable future, managed steelhead rivers are the way to successful seasons and I for one say, "the more the merrier!" As long as the Great Lakes forage base holds up, it's just sound fisheries practice.

Michigan

Beginning on the west coast (Lake Michigan) of Michigan's lower peninsula the **Platte River,** Benzie County, continues to pump out hundreds, if not thousands of steelhead for both spring and fall anglers. There are two distinct seasons on the Platte. The part of the river below Platte Lake is open year round angling. But, upstream regions close December 31 to April 1st. If you wait for the traditional opener on the river's lower reaches you'll miss the boat entirely.

Shortly after ice out on Platte Bay, thousands of silver fish run into and out of the river. The action in the rivermouth region and immediately upstream begins early with steelheaders reaping the harvest in March. Because of gin-clear water conditions on the lower river it's a UL paradise. Light Leaders coupled with buoyant spawn, single eggs or wigglers are the keys to limit catches.

Betsie River, Benzie County continues to be one of the most popular early run rivers in Michigan. Steelhead usually begin moving here in early March and provide good fishing till April 30th. The region below Homestead Dam to the Clay Banks downstream is productive waters. Also fishermen should try the Meadows near Elberta just after ice-out. Nuggets, yarn flies and wigglers are top baits here.

Big Manistee River, Manistee County, is definitely the place to be once the silver horde shows below Tippy Dam. Action begins in early April and peaks the third week. The fish, however, hang around till mid May. The bottom of the Big M. is snag-filled, so anglers float wigglers to avoid hangups. Spawn is also productive in downstream holes/lies like Suicide Bend, River Boat and Tunk Hole. Since Tippy generates power from 11:00 a.m. till 1:30 p.m. and from 5:30 p.m. to early morning this is *not* the time to fish. Low water periods are best and anglers should concentrate on probing the rivers when the "wheels"/generators are down.

Little Manistee River, Manistee County. From the DNR weir downstream to the village of Stronach on Manistee Lake the Little M. gives up many steelhead to anglers using heavy tackle and strong-arm tactics. The river here is a nightmarish jumble of logs and stumps so the UL trouter has a tough time of it. But, in the rivermouth region (at Stronach) on Manistee Lake this quickly changes. UL steelheaders rigged with bobbers and surfing outfits have in recent seasons reaped the harvest of silver migrants. They've been so successful that fisheries officials are thinking of closing this area during peak migration periods. Until they do, it remains a showplace for bending rods.

Muskegon River, Newaygo County. From the dam site at Croton downstream to the city of Muskegon the "River of Marshes" gives up good to excellent catches of *big* steelhead, both spring and fall. This is primarily boat water, but wading fishermen are able to work a number of downstream areas below Croton. The public launch 3 miles below the dam is prime spawning water and attracts both fish and fishermen in sizeable numbers.

Grand River and **Tributaries,** Kent County. From the 6th Street Dam (off Monroe St.) downtown Grand Rapids, to upstream tributaries, the Grand produces hundreds of steelhead every season for anglers willing to share the river and the bounty. At the dam face migrating rainbows pile up, then move across the spillway until they find the fish ladder on the west shore. This is a showplace for urban angling and with hundreds of thousands of fingerlings planted each year the river continues to yield good to excellent catches. The only problem with this site is high water. The Grand drains an enormous watershed and many times high water causes bank/wade fishermen to miss the migration entirely. When this happens steelheaders hit upstream tribs like the **Rogue River** (near Rockford) or **Prairie Creek** (south of Highway 21 near Ionia). Both rivers have dams blocking the steelheads upstream movement. The waters immediately below the dams and downstream gravel stretches produce good to excellent action.

St. Joe River, Berrien County. Like the Grand River the St. Joe drains an enormous watershed and when spring rains come the river rises accordingly. A cartopper with a reliable outboard will get you into fishing below the dam at Berrien Springs. Or you can show up early for the few spots of wadeable water further downstream. The river supports a very good run of fish every spring and fall with an equal compliment of boaters chasing them. Spawn, plugs and winged bobbers are popular offerings here.

Lake Huron

The east coast of Michigan's lower peninsula provides good bets for both spring and fall steelhead. Beginning at its northernmost point, the **Carp River,** Mackinac County, near St. Ignace hosts a good run of fish every season. The **Cheboygan,** Cheboygan County near Rodgers City and the

Thunder Bay River, Alpena County are both good choices for mid April. Another popular April hotspot is the **Au Sable River,** Iosoc County, particularly that stretch below Foote Dam. Since Foote is a hydro dam site and low water periods are most productive. UL steelheaders dominate fishing below the dam and the most popular baits here are wigglers, spawn, mini nuggets and single eggs. The river is a hotspot at times, then tapers off rapidly. Depending on planting success this fishery can be either boom or bust. Prime time is early April to mid May.

The **East Branch of The AuGres,** between Tawas and AuGres plus the **Rifle River,** near Omer, (Arenac County) are popular with Thumb region steelheaders. It's close-in angling and the UL artist has to use finesse to land his prize.

Upper Peninsula

At the top of Lake Michigan, **Thompson Creek,** Schoolcraft County, near Manistique is the traditional starting point for fall steelheading across the Great Lakes. The hatchery facility on Thompson Creek plants an early-run strain of Alaskan coho (silvers) and when these fish home on creek waters, the steelhead aren't far behind. This is surfing country at its best. Properly rigged the angler here can avoid the swarming salmon and take only silver torpedos in the 10 pound class. Late September to early October are prime times. On the Michigan side the Big Cedar River on Green Bay is well known for both spring and fall fish.

New York

Lake Ontario is by far the largest contributor to the steelheading that occurs in the Empire State. Both the **Little Salmon** and **Salmon Rivers,** Oswego County produce spring rainbows, but the Salmon at Pulaski gets the most attention. It's an aesthetically pleasing river with the gentle riffle, run, pool cross section of classic trout water, but that's where the similarity ends. River hotpots/lies such as Tressel, Sportsman's Pool, Black Hole and School House continually yield big steelhead to anglers willing to work under pressure. Another N.Y. hotspot is the **Niagara River** from Lake Erie on up to the Falls. These fish are lunkers also, fattened on chum fattened on chum produced in the turbines at Niagara. produced in the turbines at Niagara. Winter fish are available for both wading and boating fishermen.

Ontario

In the early days Ontario's steelheading programs were centered in the northern drainages on Lake Superior, but in recent years interest has moved south into the Georgian Bay Region of both Lakes Huron and Ontario. Like Michigan, Ontario has put the emphasis where fishermen are, thus urban steelheading has become a way of life. The waterways throughout southern Ontario are primarily spate rivers (flow determined by rainfall) and depending whether or not a stream gets adequate rains, the fishing can be either boom or bust. A reliable contact in the region is essential to catching on. Streams to watch in the **Lake Huron, Georgian Bay** region include the Beaver, Big Head, Nottawasaga, Maitland and Saugeen Rivers.

Wisconsin

Although I can not sing praises to all waters in the Badger State anglers can expect to find good steelheading in these Lake Michigan streams/rivers, both spring and fall: the **Ahnapee River,** Kewaunee County, near Forestville and the **Kewaunee River** at Kewaunee. Both are good bets early and late. The **Bear, Hibbards** and **Stony Creek,** Door County, are prime targets in peninsula country. The **Root River,** Racine County, near Milwaukee is a popular spot for urban anglers, as is the **Manitowoc,** Manitowoc County, at Manitowoc. **Lake Superior** waters include famous **Brule River,** near Brule and the Cranberry near Ashland, Wisconsin.

PACIFIC NORTHWEST
Washington

Mention the state of Washington and there's a rush of river names synonymous with the sport of steelheading . . . **Skykomish, Kalama, Stillaguamish, Washougal.** The fishery department in the Chinook State lists more than 160 streams open to *anadromous* rainbows during the winter season (running from December to March) and as one might imagine there are plenty of anglers devoting most if not all their free time to pursuing silver bullets. After the

Figure 45.   Bullet-shaped summer steelhead provide excellent action in Pacific Northwest streams, but winter fish dominate here.

devastating eruption of Mt. St. Helens (1981), the Toutle, Cowlitz and surrounding watershed are slowly mending — a tribute to mother natures endless bounty. But, it will be decades before the fishery, if ever, returns to normal. Yet, nearby the **Olympic Peninsula,** rivers continue to pump out superior numbers of sea run fish, followed by the **Puget Sound Streams** and the **Columbia** System coming in third.

Steelheaders looking for both numbers and size, the **Skagit,** Skagit County near Burlington is the place to be. In the peninsula region, the **Chehalis,** Lewis County, **Dungeness,** Clallam Co. and **Nisqually River,** Thurston Co. are consistent producers of winter fish.

The big draw for steelheaders in the Evergreen State are summer-run fish and every July hundreds of rainbow chasers from around the globe converge on Washington to pursue these jumping jacks. Fish and Game Officials list nearly 40 rivers containing Skamanian strain rainbows. These steelhead begin showing in May or June and the migration continues into October.

In the **Columbia System** best bets for summer fish include the Columbia and its tributaries: the **Klichitat, Snake, Washougal, Grand Ronde, Kalama** and **Wind.** Look for early run fish in the following **Pudget Sound Rivers — Skykomish, Tolt, Stillaguamish,** and **Snoqualmie.** In the Olympic Region look to the **Sol Duc,** Challam County, **Queets,** Jefferson County and the **Quinault River,** Jefferson and Grays Harbor County.

Oregon

As one would imagine the immense **Columbia River System** on Oregon's northern border provides both summer and winter steelheading activity for sportsmen in the Beaver State. Beginning near Portland, **Eagle Creek,** a tributary of the **Clackamas River,** winter steelhead are available from December through February.

Further inland anglers find good action on the **John Day River,** Gilliam Co.; the **Lower Umatilla** and **Imnaha Rivers,** Umatilla and Wallowa Counties; also the **Grande Ronde,** Wallowa Co. On the main Columbia, near the town of Boardman, steelheaders stack up below McNary Dam. Another productive tributary is the **Willamette River,** Yamhill and Clackmas Counties. Both boat and waders concentrate their efforts in the Oregon City Falls region of the **Willamette.** The action here runs through April.

Coastal winter waters (Dec.-Feb.) in the Clatsop, Columbia, Tillamook and Washington County areas include the **Nehalem, Wilson,** and **Trask Rivers.** Further south near Depoe Bay the **Siletz;** the **Alsea** at Alsea; **Siuslau,** west of Eugene—all are fine prospects for winter fish. Inland, east of Reedsport flows the **Umpqua** and **Smith,** both rivers synonymous with flyroddings fines. In the coast ranges, south of Coquille, look to the South Fork of the **Coquille, Rogue-Illinois, Elk** (near Port Orford) and **Chetco River** north of Brookings.

Steelheaders looking for action from October through mid March should concentrate on the northeast waters such as the **Snake, Wallowa, Imnaha** and **Grande Ronde.** In the northwest the **Santiam River** becomes active in March and gets hot in April to May. The **Hood River's** summer fish (at Hook River) peak from May to June. The summer steelhead in Oregon's famous **Deschutes River** run from May to October with the peak occuring in August to September.

California

The trouter from the Golden State is usually a salmon and steelheader, particularly if he fishes freshwater. For some the salmon, the Chinook, is still king in the Pacific Coast Range, but where steelhead run the same rivers *gairdneri* is hailed as being the ultimate in sport angling. Dams, poor lumbering practices and chemical pollution are constant threats to spawning migrations and with the current population crunch California is experiencing serious water shortages which could affect fish movements.

Steelheaders wanting to pursue silver migrants in the Central Valley region have the **Sacramento River** near Redding to consider. Before the Shasta Dam was built this watershed was unpredictable (warm in summer and flooding in winter), but now there's a salmon or steelhead run on the stream throughout the year.

In the Far North, the **Klamath** is *the* steelhead river of the drainages located near the Oregon border. Throughout its course the stream is huge, and when fishing the giant waterway one is constantly intimidated by its turbulent currents. From Clear Creek, Happy Camp, Seiad Valley, to Somesbar the **Klamath** gives up fish to anglers willing to probe its secretive waters.

For the less adventuresome, steelheaders should concentrate on northwestern Del Norte Counties' **Smith River** (long famous for big Chinook Salmon) or the **Eel River,** Lake County. Humboldt County has the famous **Matthole, Mad** and **Redwood Rivers** for the angler to explore. Inland streams in Trinity County include the **Trinity, Scott, Salmon, Hayfork** and **Van Duzen.** The list goes on and on. Most of the creeks and rivers in northern and coastal regions are primarily salmon and steelhead waters and if you've got the time and energy, I'm certain you'll find your pot of gold — hopefully at the end of a rainbow.

CHAPTER 13
TYING STEELHEAD FLY PATTERNS AND TACKLE MISCELLANY

Steelheaders attempting to apply traditional trouting rational to present day *anadromous* rainbow fly patterns will find themselves awash in a sea of non-conformity. When this escape from parochial thinking took place is open to speculation, but I suspect it was brought on by the likes of Jim Pray, an enterprising and inventive fly tier and steelheader from Eureka, California. Back in the 40's Pray's angling philosophy was simple . . . "suit the fish, then the fisherman." By adding large, brass bead-chain eyes to his hot innovations (later known as Pray's Optics) Jim was able to put his fly on bottom quickly and take fish. The fact that the pattern had no standard tail, wing, hackle, nor suggested any known insect form was secondary to the fact that the fly dredged up steelhead after steelhead from his beloved Fernbridge Pool.

Today that same adventuresome attitude is alive and well among the ranks of the ultra light steelheader using flies both here in the midwest and Pacific northwest. Anglers in these regions are not willing to accept the defeat easily. If steelhead can't be taken by standard methods/leaders, baits and rigs, they experiment. By adopting such attitudes the evolution of methodology is more fluid. Instead of dwelling on past victories they work to establish new techniques. If tradition doesn't pay off they examine season, water color, (turbidity) river levels, temperature and hour of the day and apply it to their success. By using knowledge our steelheading is being examined as never before. And as you might imagine facts are revealing misconceptions.

When I began serious steelheading back in the early 70's standard fare for spring fish was tiny spawn sacs meshed in orange gauze. A few years later an inquisitive rainbow chaser from Capac, Michigan, Burl Brown introduced plastic mini nugget (imitation spawn) made of a polymer similar to that used in bass'n worms and steelhead jumped on them in a big way. As Burl said . . . "if they'll eat worms, they'll eat plastic," and for the most part he was right. Today, plastics are used to fashion mayfly nymphs, spawn bags, lures and as wing and body material for a number of fly patterns. Actually the material is a spun polypropolene yarn, but it is, none the less, "plastic."

The discovery that steelhead had a natural affinity toward fluorescent fly colors further set the traditionalist on a downward path of swooning, yet for the technician such data simply meant a better way and often less expensive way of building a mousetrap. Today, if it can be wrapped on a hook and casts easily and takes fish, then it is included in the anglers bag of tricks called flies.

In Chapter 6, I covered the technical aspects of using flies and told why (theoretically) these bits of fur, feather and steel are so effective in taking spring and fall fish. Here, I want to give the UL angler the How To of building standard fly patterns including: a. Spring Nymph (wiggler) b. Yarn fly (attractor) c. Wiggle nymph (*Hexagenia*) and d. Stonefly nymphs, plus the rational behind each pattern — why it's effective and the best time to use the pattern. I recognize there are other "successful" patterns for steelheading, so I've included my list of "12 Best" selections for midwestern streams. By employing the basic tying instructions for the 4 patterns, any of the Standard/Traditional flies can be fashioned.

Spring Nymph (Wiggler)

Head Color:	Depends on body color-black, brown or green
Body:	Medium chenille, colors include: yellow, beige, green, hot pink, burnt & hot orange, green, gray
Hackle:	Ginger saddle hackle, Palmered
Tail:	Fox Squirrel (fawn beige color)
Back/Wing:	Fox Squirrel
Hook:	2 or 3 X long, Size 6, 8

The basic pattern for this fly was cooked up by Ron Spring, a sporting goods dealer from Muskegon, Michigan, and is perhaps the most popular of the flies used to mimic the giant mayfly *(Hexagenia limbata)* found in most Michigan steelhead rivers. Depending on water level and turbidity this pattern is run in a variety of body colors, with no single color dominating the UL steelheaders fly box. In late March early April, I prefer natural colors to attract fish prior to spawning, like beige, brown, green and yellow. Actually, the color of the natural Hex nymph is a straw colored beige or yellow, so any hue mimicking the real thing is usually effective. Fish these "on bottom" and hit the fish on the nose. When waters are discolored or in early morning I run fluorescent bodied nymphs. The hot colors get the most attention simply because the fly is more visible to holding fish.

How To Tie

Start the thread immediately behind hook eye and wind clock-wise down the shank. This serves as a foundation for the body so keep the wraps even. Directly above hook point attach a clump of fox squirrel, extending it beyond the hook bend. This forms the tail. Now secure the saddle hackle directly in front of the tail. Be sure to wind enough thread at

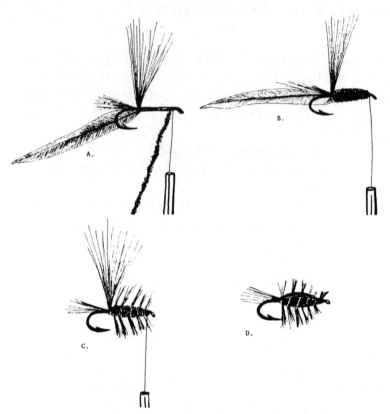

Figure 46. Tying procedure for SPRING NYMPH. Use variety of body colors for best coverage.

the base of the tail to set the tail fibers at right angles to the hook shank.

Wind the thread forward to hook eye and attach a 3 inch section of medium chenille. Wrap the body material down the shank and back. This double layer fills out the body nicely and creates a tapered affair. Tie off. Now, wind the hackle forward (palmer style & clock-wise) and tie off behind the eye. Finally, pull the squirrel tail forward over the body creating a "shelled" nymph back. Tie off the butt fibers just behind the eye. Make a pronounced head and varnish or lacquer. If you wish, lacquer the back section several times. The fly will not only last longer, but has a realistic nymph look.

Yarn Fly

Just when and where the yarn fly got its start is open to speculation, but it is no doubt a west coast innovation. For years steelheaders there snelled colorful yarn balls to baited setups, and with the introduction of poly yarns the science of yarn flies has taken a new twist. I use these bits of fluff in early morning when steelhead are aggressively territorializing. In the right color combinations of hot pink, chartreuse and orange they are highly effective. Matter of fact they are so effective most mid-season steelheaders would not be on the stream without a good supply. They only take minutes to make and the cost is the best part, about 4 cents each. Since steelheading does take a high toll of terminal tackle, yarn flies can be the savior for the angler with a thin wallet.

Thread Color: Depending on yarn color, yellow or red
Hook: 5 x stout bait hook, Size 6, 8, 10 bronze or gold
Body: Spun poly yarn — yellow, orange, pink, red, chartreuse, etc.

By visiting your local knit shop you can secure enough poly yarn to make thousands of flies, in a variety of colors. The hair ties popularized by young girls are also another good source of poly material. If there's a tackle shop nearby

Figure 47.   Yarn flies are standard fare for spring fish. Use fluorescent colors throughout.

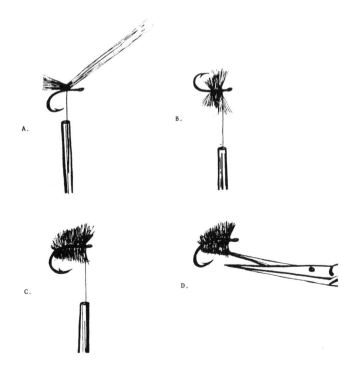

Luhr Jensen supplies convenient 20 yard spools of poly yarn and the cost is reasonable.

Start the thread immediately behind the hook eye. Run it back to a point opposite the barb. Since poly yarn comes in various sizes you'll have to separate a section that will produce a nicely tapered fly.

The yarn sectioned, place it on top of the hook shank. Secure with two winds, then one in front. Now turn the hook upside down and repeat the process. The second yarn clump is added in front of the first, then duplicated on bottom. After three or four bunches the fly should take on a sac (circular) appearance. Fill the shank completely and tie off just behind the eye. I generally add a bit of hot orange or red just behind the eye. Whether it makes a difference or not is debatable, but I add it anyway. Once the fly is completed you may trim to shape or leave fluffy.

A second method of yarn attachment is similar to that used to create deer hair bass bugs and for lack of a better term it's called spinning. After cinching down the first yarn clump, run the tying thread through the fiber, thus spinning the "plastic" onto the shank. Repeat the entire process top to bottom until a "ball" is created. Either method is fine and the results are top drawer.

Wiggle Nymph

This fly pattern is extremely effective during mid and late season steelheading when water levels are low and the fish are finicky (easily spooked). As mentioned in Chapter 6—Steelheading with Flies, the nymph is articulated in the middle, thus mimicking naturals in the family *Ephemerellidae*. In their excellent book "Selective Trout" Doug Swisher and Carl Richards show a version of the "wiggle" nymph and although it's a very effective fly, it isn't the easiest pattern to tie.

The wiggle nymph I use for steelhead is a take off on the Swisher/Richards pattern, but only two materials are needed to create it — a red squirrel tail and the gray fili-plume feather from a Ruff grouse. It is a suggestive rather than realistic pattern, but I've taken steelhead with this fly when they would only strike *Hexagenia* nymphs.

Head:	Pronounced (full) either beige or black thread
Hooks:	3 x long Alcott bait hook (for tail section) Size 12 Wide Bend Eagle Claw No. 42, Size 12 (body section)
Tail:	Reddish-beige red squirrel tail
Body:	Palmered grouse filiplume feather, gray
Hackle:	Ruff grouse breast feather or red squirrel
Shell Back:	Red Squirrel pulled forward

Place the Alcott or similar bait hook in vise and straighten (the offset portion of hook is lined up with shank). Run thread evenly down hook shank. Clip small clump of squirrel and tie in opposite barb. The tail should extend half hook length beyond bend. Wind thread at tail base and set fibers at right anglers (this will be shell backed later). Now,

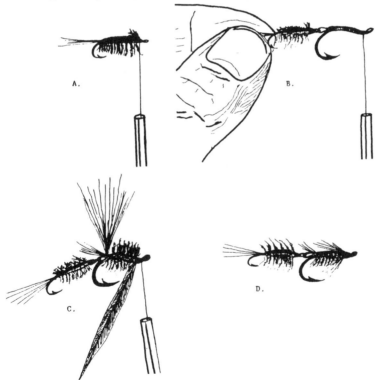

Figure 48. Wiggle nymphs often trigger vicious strikes. Perhaps the BEST low water fly.

attach the filiplume feather (each breast feather has a single filiplume attached to its base, so look for it). Select one that is about 1" long and palmer forward. Tie off. Now pull the squirrel tail forward and tie off. The gray filiplume feather creates very realistic gills which undulate in river currents.

Clip a 4 inch section of 6 lb-test mono and run it through the eye of the tail segment (this forms the hinge). Place the wide-bend Eagle Claw in the vise and wind the tying thread down the shank. Position the tail section with mono on top of the shank and secure with several thread wraps. Then, Super Glue the mono to the hook. Using this method of attachment, I've taken steelhead on the rear hook! Tough!

The body portion is created exactly like the tail, but shorten tail overhang. After pulling the squirrel forward, form a large head and lacquer both head and shell back. The basic idea is to have the tail hinge up and down freely, so watch this carefully. A correctly tied wiggle nymph is so effective it actually turns fish on. I've had rainbows chase and engulf a fluttering nymph. Motion is the key to success here.

Stone Fly Nymphs

During the height of nest building rainbows dislodge a number of large stoneflies in both *Taeniopteryx* and *Pteronarcys* groups and addressing males below a redd area pick up these drifting morsels. Whether they are feeding instinctively or protecting territory is a matter for fish biologists to discuss. I do know stonefly nymphs work extremely well. So well, in fact, they have top billing in my fly book, during both early and late season. In order to simplify the stonefly pattern I use two materials . . . slate gray rabbit fur and grizzly hackle. You can get a little more sophisticated, but I've found it unnecessary. Tie a few nymphs using my pattern, then go your own route. Like most steelhead patterns, the simpler they are the better they are.

I tie this pattern on Mustads TUE No. 36890, Black Salmon hook sizes 8 & 10. Run tying thread to point opposite hook point. The sparser you tie this fly the quicker it gets down. Strip a few short hackle fibers and attach tail. Tie in a

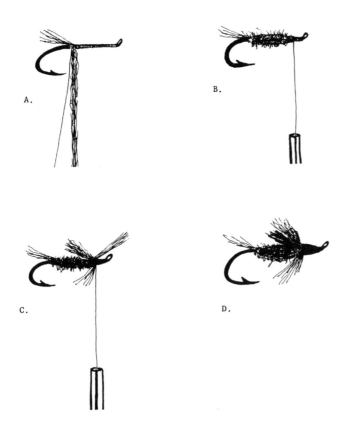

Figure 49.   Stoneflies are tops for selective steelheading in late season.
Size 8 and 10 are standard.

Figure 50. Deadly Dozen: Top steelhead flies in Midwest. (Left - Right, Top - Bottom) Spring Nymphs, pink chartreuse and orange bodies, Size 6; Doctor Rex, Size 6; P.M. Sunrise, No. 6; Mickey Finn Streamer, No. 4; Comet, Size 6; Black Bear, green butt, No. 6; Skunk, No. 6; Double Egg Sac Fly, No. 6; Single Egg, Hot Orange and Pink, Size 8.

two inch section of fine copper wire for rib. Dub dun-gray fur on thread, spin and then wind on shank. Repeat until a tapered body is achieved. Wind copper ribbing forward and tie off. (The fine wire rib strengthens and toughens a dubbed body considerably and is good for holding steelhead flies together.)

Thread:	Black nymph (flat)
Body:	Dubbed gray rabbit fur, tapered
Tail:	Grizzly hackle fibers
Rib:	fine copper wire
Wing pad:	Grizzly
Hackle:	Grizzly

Strip a small clump of Grizzly hackle fibers and attach at wind pad area. If you choose, underlay this pad with a small bunch of black poly yarn, making the wing stand out. I don't know if it makes any difference, so you be the judge. All flies are a reflection of their maker. If you think it makes a difference use it. Now reverse the hook, tie in the throat hackle and finish with a nicely tapered head.

OF VESTS AND THINGS

In this segment I'd like to cover a number of items which are near and dear to most steelheaders, but for one reason or another don't get covered in print. They include vests, boots, gear for organizing terminal setups, ways of preserving and presenting steelhead or salmon eggs, plus knots for all seasons. I learned a long time ago when fish are doing it there's no place for fumbling fingers and lost patience. The organized steelheader is the successful steelheader.

Vests

Like most anglers my first vest for steelheading was a retread from earlier flyfishing days. With multiple pockets I was able to cover the field completely, but as you might suspect the thing weighed a ton. A long day on the river I felt like an oxen in yoke. After more than my share of stiff necks I went to the drawing board and with a little help from the wife I came up with a "shorty" vest of UL proportions.

Basically, it has a front and back with a total of 5 pockets, plus a fly book and drying pad. All closures are velcro and the best part of the deal is the weight. Fully loaded it pulls the scale down a mere 3 pounds!

The front pockets are long and accommodate a pair of stack caps (for hooks, split shot, corkies, three-way swivels) flex light, bobbers and reel wrench. They also house a generous supply of plastic spawn and single eggs. The fly book holds a basic fly selection for immediate use. The back pocket is large enough to handle a shorty rain jacket. The two inside pockets hold a stream thermometer and extra leader wheels in 2 and 4 pound-test.

If I want to extend my vest's capabilities I add a fly chest made from two Perrine flyboxes pop riveted together. In the compartmented box I tote additional terminal gear, including Colorado spinners, two way swivels, fine split shot, lead wire, etc. The fly box holds a generous supply of the four basic fly patterns, plus a selection of the "deadly dozen." If you don't have a seamstress available to cook up an UL vest I suggest purchasing a Shorty vest and modify it to suit your needs. A couple of elastic loops to hold bobbers is usually all that's needed.

Boots and Waders

I'm sure you've heard the adage about "cold hands, warm heart," but when love's away and you're on a steelhead river, cold hands are the net result of cold feet and it goes downhill from there. Typically the coldest most miserable conditions come during the hottest fishing and for those anglers able to brave the slings and arrows of outrageous storms, limit catches are the rule rather than the exception.

Over the years I've more than paid my dues to weather master and after going through more than 15 cold springs and falls I think I can offer some frank advice on dressing for steelheading. Since I'm not promoting a particular wader manufacturer, I'll simply say buy the best insulated boot foot wader you can afford. If you wear an 8½ buy size 9. This will allow you to wear a pair of insulated Bamma socks by Royal. This is the best innovation to come

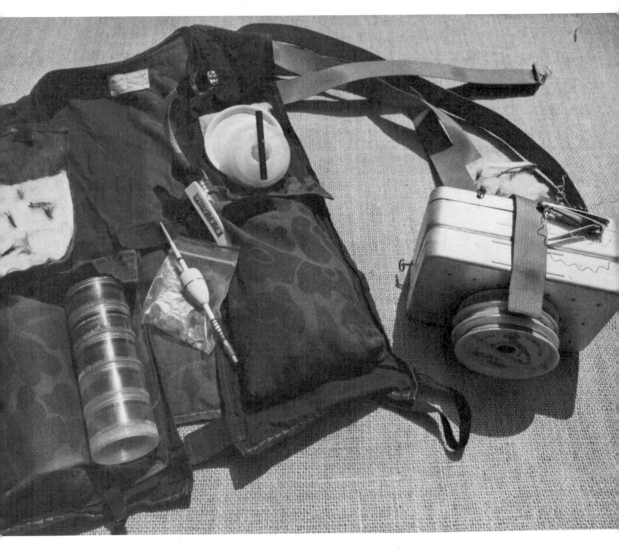

Figure 51. Shorty steelhead vest has ample room for stack caps, bobbers, nuggets, leader wheels, flex light. Weight, 3½ lbs.

along in years. The sock wicks away foot moisture and holds it there. I take two pair along, wearing one while the other dries. Socks can be wool or cotton. By wearing a medium weight you'll be set for hours.

If you'll be standing in water above the thighs wear a pair of quality long johns, wool or polypropolene. Next comes a heavy pair of wool pants. Wool holds body heat even when filled with perspiration and when you take the wader off the garment feels dry. Top off the whole affair with a wool cap, a down coat and you'll be able to brave the worst of elements.

Spawn Sacs and Preservation

There are times when steelhead will only strike skein spawn or spawn bags tied from freshly prepared single eggs. I'd never think of going stream side without a good supply of both. It's just good business to do so. Preparing both single eggs and skein spawn is easy and takes only a few minutes (see Chapter 7 for formula). A final note — if you prepare spawn bags experiment with nylon mesh color. On my last trip to the Manistee River I had chartreuse, hot orange and hot pink sacs and on that particular day (dark, rainy and overcast) hot pink was the ticket. I guess it pays to be prepared.

Knots

The Improved Clinch Knot ranks as one of the all time favorites and one of the most widely used knots today. Although not as strong as some of the newer knots, it still provides an easy, quick connection with good strength. When tied properly the angler can achieve up to 75-80% of original line strength. Use 7 wraps with lines under 17 lb-test, and a minimum of 5 on lines above 17.

The Trilene Knot is recommended for use with all premium nylon monofilaments. It is very similar to the Improved Clinch, but with a double loop through the eye. Connections on snaps, swivels, hooks and lures, particularly with UL gear it's ideal. The unique design and ease of tying yields strong dependable knots of 85-90% of original pound test. The double wrap provides a cushion and added safety factor for light lines.

Figure 52. Using spawn bag machine steelheader can turn out sacs with variety of mesh colors to suit water conditions.

1

2

3

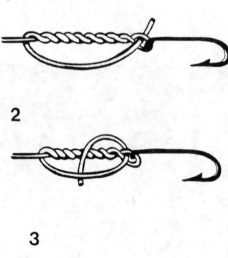

Figure 53. IMPROVED CLINCH KNOT (Dwgs courtesy Berkley & Co.)

Figure 54. TRILENE KNOT (Dwgs courtesy Berkley & Co.)

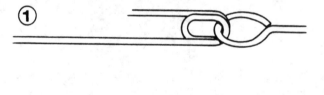

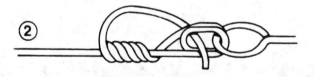

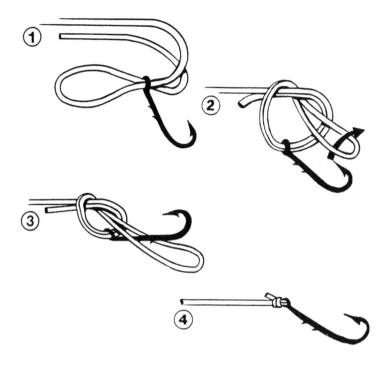

Figure 55.   PALOMAR KNOT (Dwg. courtesy Berkley & Co.)

The Palomar Knot is recommended for use with quality monos. It is simple to tie and like the Trilene Knot provides a cushion for light lines. As with the Clinch and Trilene knots moisten with saliva before cinching down. 85 to 90% of original line strength is maintained if tied properly.

CHAPTER 14
THOUGHTS ON STEELHEADING — PAST, PRESENT AND FUTURE

MIDWEST
Michigan

A lot of water has passed under the bridge since those first steelhead fry were received at the Big Rapids, Michigan Hatchery from New York's Caledonia facility. The year was 1885 and this was still another chapter in the continuing saga of the "silvery trout" from California. Between 1876 and 1895 numerous plants had been made in rivers draining Michigan's west coast, yet the program never seemed to click. Shortly after that spring introduction in the amber waters of the Pere Marquette River, the young steelhead migrated to Lake Michigan, "not to be seen again!" Locals called the project a failure from the beginning. A few of the new immigrants were taken during the summer of 1885, but that was it.

From time to time big, lake-fattened rainbows showed in the nets of commercial operators working Lake Michigan waters, and their discovery attracted the attention of Frank Clark, then a biologist at the Northville Hatchery near Detroit, Michigan. Clark long suspected these big trout were decendents of earlier river plants, and with good reason. Since traditional river angling ended in September, long before steelhead began fall migratory runs, it was entirely possible the rainbows simply escaped detection. Years passed before Michigan officials realized they'd created a lasting steelhead fishery in the Great Lakes.

In 1904 Frank Clark began experimenting with pure steelhead strains and subsequently introduced their progeny into Great Lakes waters. What followed is a matter of history. As these plants took hold, the fishery flourished in rivers such as the Platte, Betsie, Pere Marquette, Big and Little Manistee and Au Sable. Word quickly spead across the U.S. and it wasn't long before anglers were traveling thousands of miles to reap the harvest of big lake-run fish.

Then, in 1940 the entire program came unravelled. Completion of the Welland Canal brought with it the dreaded sea lamprey and nuisance alewife. During WW II the demand for fish products increased dramatically, and it wasn't long before set gill nets reduced fish stocks dramatically. Literally overnight the ecology of the Big Lakes were irrevocably altered.

It wasn't until 1957 that an effective lampricide was found. A selective compound called TFM killed larval ammocetes in headwater gravel and it wasn't long before the big anadromous rainbows staged a strong comeback.

To augment the re-building program the Michigan Department of Natural Resources implemented plans for new hatchery construction for rearing both brown trout and steelhead. Similar programs were also launched in neighboring states/provinces like Wisconsin, Indiana, Minnesota and Ontario.

Eighteen years later the DNR is still continuing applied research and nutrition of steelhead with the same fervor that characterized the "early" days and to date annual plantings in the Great Lakes alone total several million smolts.

As mentioned in Chapters 1 and 2 there are those in the steelheading community that consider hatchery fish as being inferior to wild ones, both genetically and physically, and I suspect they are correct, yet the Michigan DNR, like other steelheading states, are faced with a dilemma. On the one hand they must supply a constant/uninterrupted supply of migrating rainbows to an intensely used fishery, or face the gradual depletion of wild fish stocks.

When the Department rejected use of the Great Lakes as an industrial fishery and opted to aggressively launch a program of restoration, they in effect welcomed the "hatchery" policy with open arms. Even if they wanted to return to the old days, they are so committed to the new direction there is no turning back. Indeed, in many instances so many of the rivers in the lower peninsula have been damaged so badly (enviromentally) they could no longer sustain healthy stocks of wild fish, even if such stocks could somehow be re-introduced.

Fortunately, many of our northwest Michigan rivers still maintain wild, self-sustaining populations/runs of fish and I for laud the DNR for continuing a hands-off policy. Hopefully, these crystalline waters may one day provide a showcase for emulation statewide. It will be a long way down the road, but why set our sights low and expect less.

Presently, Michigan's steelhead program is a bright spot on an otherwise clouded national scene. With the help of fishery people in the Hoosier State (Indiana) we've currently introduced the summer-run Skamania Strain (named for Washington States' Skamanian River Hatchery facility) steelhead in several lower peninsula rivers including the Muskegon, Pere Marquette, and Manistee Rivers (Big and Little) plus the Au Sable River on Lake Huron.

Introduced in spring 84, fisheries staffers expect a partial return of summer fish in 85 and 86 and a full blown migration in the third year. Actually the Michigan plants are a variety of summer-run fish including the Siletz steelhead (planted in the White River-Lake Mich. & Chocolay River-Lake Superior), Umpqua River variety (planted in the Muskegon and Pere Marquette Rivers) and Rogue River strain (introduced in the Manistee, Betsie, Boyne and Au

Sable Rivers). At the present, Lake Michigan tributaries are scheduled to recieve 156,000 fish while the Chocolay will get 20,000, and the Au Sable 47,000. If only a fraction of the plants return it will be difficult to access the programs' success, yet steelheaders statewide are optimistic.

"We've wanted this summer-run fish for a long time now," states Ray Schmidt, President and founder of the newly organized Steelheaders Anglers Society, Manistee, Mich. "There have been problems with plant sites and premature harvest of young fish, but every new program has it's ups and downs." It may take as many as 5 to 10 years before a full blown Skamanian program is established on Lake Michigan, but for the dedicated steelheader it's a management program worth waiting for!

Indiana

Before the introduction of summer-run steelhead in Hoosier waters, Indiana had little to offer the angling public. With vast acres of Lake Michigan real estate open to fishermen in the Gary, Michigan City and Chicago area, the waters there were, at best, a temporary fishery. After lake shallows warmed into the 60's schooled steelhead and salmon simply migrated north to cooler Michigan waters. Shoals which had earlier yielded salmonid catches once again became a watery desert frequented only by bass and perch fishermen.

Of the tributaries Indiana has to offer steelheaders, few if any can be loosely classified as trout streams. Most are irrigation ditches grown over, with limited or no public access. Yet, it was against such a management backdrop that fisheries officials imprinted traditional steelhead stocks in southern Lake Michigan. This program continued for a full decade with mediocre success. That's when DNR biologists began experimenting with the Skamanian rainbow from Washington.

On paper the fish looked promising. Their migrations occurred during early summer. The homing instinct was strong and the adults entered river waters in mid to late summer when stream temperatures were high. Since spawning didn't take place until late winter (Feb. to March) the staging period in lake waters would be long and hopefully successful. In the 5th year 200,000 yearlings were introduced in southern Lake Michigan with an equal number to follow annually.

In the third year, it was the adults that stole the show in the big Lake. All up and down the Michigan City shoreline the silvery, lean torpedos exploded from the surface waters much to the delight of trolling steelheaders. Even though this fishery is of the downrigger or flat line variety, UL steelheaders here are breaking records every year on 2 and 4 pound-test lines. Since Indiana has the only available supply of eggs in the world, there is a waiting list that grows larger each season. What the future holds is anyone's guess, but for now Indiana rainbow chasers are having the time of their lives.

Wisconsin

Without abundant estuarial waters for migrating steelhead to ascend, the Badger State is faced with a dilemma similar to Indiana . . . "Traditional plants are not working, so experiment." According to DNR officials, current plants of 1 ½ million fish are only yielding 25 to 30 thousand fish, and . . ." that's not what we'd like." Apparently the Michigan and California Shasta strains of steelhead are not doing it, so it's back to the drawing board.

Recently the fisheries division introduced 70,000 Indiana Skamania to the Oconto River, at Green Bay and another 30,000 to the Root, near Racine. Other waterways are scheduled for future plants, but for now anglers will have to take a wait and see attitude.

Like Michigan, Wisconsin's plants are totally dependent on the supply of eggs provided by the Indiana program, so this exciting fishery may take five to ten years to develop. If it does come on line, look out Green Bay.

Against this backdrop of electrifying fishing I would be remiss if I failed to point out that all is not well in the steelheaders world. Recent reversals in Michigan's Bay Mills Indian fishing controversy has turned the clock back for anglers in the Great Lakes State. Gill nets, as they did in the days following WW II, once again threaten present fish stocks in the 5 sisters. Lake trout are the first to suffer the ravages of monofilament walls and as of this writing, the sport fishing/trolling season for *Salvelinus namaycush* has been reduced to May 1 through August 15th in Lakes Michigan, Huron and their tributaries.

Even thought salmonids like steelhead and salmon (both coho and chinook) are less susceptible to gill net operations they do account for a percentage of Indian harvest in the Great Lakes. How much is tough or impossible to determine, but on several occasions in recent springs, I've taken fish from both the Pere Marquette and Muskegon Rivers showing gill net marks on head and body areas.

Right or wrong, good or bad the question has been thrust upon us and ultimately will be won, lost or compromised in the courts, but in the meantime individual steelheaders can do their part by joining National Conservation/Cold water organizations like Trout Unlimited or regional groups within their respective states, such as Michigan's Steelhead and Salmon Fisherman's Association (MSSFA), one of the foremost guardians of salmonid management in the midwest. A working relationship with the DNR helps MSSFA establish sound fisheries policies, a key to quality sport fishing. Additionally, both organizations are intent on improving basic water quality across the entire Great Lakes basin. You can contribute significantly to the future of steelheading nationwide just by becoming involved. With numbers comes strength, and a unified voice is important to being heard in the state houses where policies are formulated.

Idaho

If midwestern steelhead problems seem tough, consider the enigma faced by silver migrants in the Gem State. The fish that ascend the Columbia and Snake systems to reach inland spawning waters on the Salmon and Clearwater Rivers are forced to negotiate a series of fish passages at hydro dams sites. Of course these facilities were built . . .

"to accommodate returning adults," but in recent years these avenues of access have become death traps, not for mature fish, but juveniles migrating downstream.

Turbines in the hydro installation chop thousands of the unsuspecting fish into chum and if they are lucky enough to escape the blades, another hazard awaits them, the "gas-bubble" disease. This results when spillway waters become supersaturated with air/nitrogen. The gases enter the fish's circulatory system, the net result is equivalent to a case of bends in deep-sea divers. Blood vessels rupture. Bubbles surface on the body and operculum. In severe cases the eyes simply explode. Faced with the prospects of no steelhead runs at all, Idaho has been forced to use "hatchery" fish to sustain traditional runs of wild steelhead.

To avoid dams and their associated problems the Army Corps of Engineers and the National Marine Fisheries Services annually conduct Operation Fish Run. Juvenile salmon and steelhead are intercepted in their downstream journey, then trucked and barged to the lower Columbia, where they can resume their migration to the sea.

The system seems to work, but when they return 3 years later as adults they must run a maze of Indian gill nets that boggles the mind. Commercial netting is designed for taking salmon, but runs overlap and the steelhead are swept away. How many are taken by netters is tough to estimate, but I'm sure it's substantial. Every year steelheaders in Idaho don't know whether they will be able to creel fish, or indeed if there is to be a season at all. When a season is announced overcrowding becomes a real problem, even on remote waters.

In Chapter 1 I did not list Idaho as a steelheading area, and given the present circumstances the fishery there needs breathing room. According to research biologists, if Operation Fish Run continues and adequate river flows generated, the long-term prospects of rebuilding steelhead stock is very real. Yet drought and increased water demand can change this optimistic picture overnight.

Like their cousins in Idaho, Washington State steelhead face similar obstacles to survival. One of them is the quality of the fish itself. Again, the argument centers on whether or not wild fish are genetically and physically superior to "hatchery" steelhead. At this point, Washington is so committed to augmenting their program with hatchery fish, I feel it's a mute question. Like Michigan, many of the rivers in the Evergreen State have been so environmentally damaged few could sustain wild fish at all. Thus may coastal fisheries have become put and take affairs.

A second and perhaps more critical problem centers on the Indian Fishery. In 1970 the federal government acting as a trustee for Indian rights filed suit against the state, claiming they had denied fishing rights granted by earlier treaties. In 1974, District Court judge George Bolt ruled the tribes were entitled to 50% of the harvestable salmon and steelhead returning to areas covered by the 1850 treaty.

Initially Indian fishermen went after salmon stocks, but in recent years runs have diminished significantly and the attention now centers on steelhead. And, as you might imagine fish numbers have declined to the point where many sportsmen no longer purchase *anadromous* licenses, arguing against funding an Indian Commercial fishery for steelhead. Right or wrong this attitude is bound to affect support of river preservation and ultimately there will be precious few fish for anyone to harvest, including Indians. At present it's difficult to be optimistic about the steelheading scene in Washington. Of course legal and legislative manuevering will continue on the issue, yet the real loser is the fish, not man.

INDEX